THE NEW TEMPLE SHAKESPEARE

Edited by M. R. Ridley, M.A.

OTHELLO

by William Shakespeare

London: J. M. DENT & SONS LTD.
New York: E. P. DUTTON & CO. INC.

Editor's General Note

The Text. The editor has kept before him the aim of presenting to the modern reader the nearest possible approximation to what Shakespeare actually wrote. The text is therefore conservative, and is based on the earliest reliable printed text. But to avoid distraction (*a*) the spelling is modernised, and (*b*) a limited number of universally accepted emendations is admitted without comment. Where a Quarto text exists as well as the First Folio the passages which occur only in the Quarto are enclosed in square brackets [ ] and those which occur only in the Folio in brace brackets { }.

Scene Division. The rapid continuity of the Elizabethan curtainless production is lost by the 'traditional' scene divisions. Where there is an essential difference of place these scene divisions are retained. Where on the other hand the change of place is insignificant the scene division is indicated only by a space on the page. For ease of reference, however, the 'traditional' division is retained at the head of the page and in line numbering.

Notes. Passages on which there are notes are indicated by a † in the margin.

Punctuation adheres more closely than has been usual to the 'Elizabethan' punctuation of the early texts. It is often therefore more indicative of the way in which the lines were to be delivered than of their syntactical construction.

Glossaries are arranged on a somewhat novel principle, not alphabetically, but in the order in which the words or phrases occur. The editor is much indebted to Mr J. N. Bryson for his collaboration in the preparation of the glossaries.

v

Preface

The Text. The First Quarto of the play appeared in 1622, probably early in the year, since the copyright was assigned to Thomas Walkley in October of 1621, and there seems no reason for securing the copyright of a play that had been on the boards so long except that of immediate publication. And one may guess that Walkley was anxious to anticipate the Folio by as long as he could. The title-page is THE / Tragœdy of Othello, / The Moore of Venice. / *As it hath beene diuerse times acted at the* / Globe, and at the Black Friers, by / *his Maiesties Seruants.* / *Written by* William Shakespeare. / *LONDON,* / Printed by N. O. for *Thomas Walkley,* and are to be sold at his / shop, at the Eagle and Child, in Brittans Bursse. / 1622. In 1627 Walkley transferred his copyright to Richard Hawkins, and the latter published the Second Quarto in 1630.

The problem of the text of the play presents certain peculiar features, and is also, I think, less plain of solution than has usually been supposed. As a rule, where a Quarto was extant, it is clear that the Folio was printed from it, with an editing sometimes slight and sometimes extensive. With this play it was unlikely, owing to the late publication of the Quarto, that this would be so; and in fact it needs only the most cursory examination of the Q and F texts to be sure that whatever the relation between them is, F was certainly not set from Q, and was certainly also set from a MS. presenting a very large number of differences from the MS. from which Q was set.

But when we come to make up our minds which of the two texts is to be regarded as the more authoritative, our difficulties begin. What may roughly be called the 'usual' view may be represented by two quotations. "In addition to many improved readings, the play as printed in the Folio contained over one hundred and fifty verses omitted in the earlier edition, while, on the other hand, ten or fifteen lines in the Quarto were not represented in the Folio version. . . . The text of modern editions of the play is based on that of the First Folio, though it is not denied that we have in the First Quarto a genuine play-house copy." "The superiority of the Folio is easily proved. In the first place, it contains about 160 lines, undoubtedly genuine, omitted in the First Quarto. Again, there are very many errors or misprints in the First Quarto which are correctly rendered by the Folio. There are indeed a certain number of important exceptions where the readings of the 1622 Quarto are better than the Folio." Now before one comes to any detailed examination of the two texts those two quotations suggest an observation which is of some importance to the general problem of Shakespearean texts. In both the presence in F of passages not present in Q is taken as a sign of 'superiority,' and is linked with an 'improvement' or 'correctness' of individual readings. But that surely is a confusion of thought; the two things have nothing essentially to do with one another. A thoroughly badly printed text of a complete MS. is in no proper sense of the word 'superior' to an accurately printed text of a 'cut' MS. It is more complete, and that is all. The 'superiority' of the one text to the other must be settled, so far as settlement is possible, by a comparison of them where they more or less coincide. And it does not at all help us to talk of 'improved' readings, unless we know who the improver was; nor, in very many cases, does it seriously help us to talk of 'correct' readings, unless we have the original in front of us. Often, of course, and particularly where one can see how the error arose, one can reasonably say that one text is right and the other wrong. In the first scene of this play, for example, when F reads *tongued consuls* or *hell apines*, where Q reads *toged consuls* and *hells paines*, one may say that Q is correct; or when Q reads *be led* or *frequent messengers* where F reads *be beleed* and *sequent messengers* one may say that F is correct. But when one text reads *For this delusion* and the other *For thus deluding you*, or one reads *Are all doores lockt* and the other *Are your doores lockt*, it is impossible to do more than conjecture which the author originally wrote, and one has regretfully to admit that which reading one prefers depends largely on one's presuppositions about the two texts. If one has determined in advance, on whatever grounds, that F or Q is the superior text, one will almost inevitably suffer from an unconscious bias in selecting between more or less indifferent readings, and in the process strengthen one's belief in the superiority of one's chosen text.

If one examines the two main texts of this play in general, one thing becomes immediately apparent. In the first place Q 1 is in the technical sense a 'good' quarto; it exhibits, that is, none of the garblings and other hall-marks of the pirated 'bad' quartos. Further, it is based on an early 'state' of the MS. of the play, certainly anterior to that Act of 1606 for restraining the abuses of the players which led to such elaborate expurgatory editing. In the second place Q 1 is based on a *stage* MS. F, on the other hand, is based on a state of the MS. of any date we choose later than 1606 (the expurgation is unusually complete), and on a state which had little reference to the theatre. We may perhaps here glance at two general differences between the two texts.

1. *Omissions.* Of these there are three classes. (*a*) Those due apparently to pure carelessness. Both texts occasionally leave out

a half line or so. (*b*) Those due to carelessness of a different kind or to misunderstanding; the compositor's eye is caught by the same or a similar word and he skips (*e.g.* III. iii. 330 (Q), iv. 94 (F)), or (this only in Q) he takes brackets to be an indication of omission (*e.g.* I. ii. 65, iii. 64). These two classes are of minor importance, and small significance. They include, I think, all the omissions of F. The third class is of much greater importance; it consists of passages omitted by Q, some of which are generally accepted as being dramatic cuts, others of which have been supposed to be additions made by Shakespeare himself; and the point is vital, since if he added passages to a play that was supposed completed, he may well have revised more extensively, not only in this play but in others. To take the passages in order. I. i. 121-37; an unessential passage of Roderigo. I. ii. 72-78; clearly, I think, a cut, since the edges are joined by reading *Such* instead of F's *For* in l. 78. I. iii. 25-31; an unessential passage of the senator. II. iii. 269-71; an odd cut; the lines are vivid, and their omission saves very little time. These might be an addition. III. iii. 388-95; an odd cut, since Iago's answer is more effective with it in; but an even odder addition. III. iii. 457-64; this is the most disputed of all the passages, the usual argument being that no one, if he had this superb passage in front of him, could conceivably cut it. But this argument seems to forget what the business of the unhappy cutter is. Somehow or other he has to shorten his play by a given number of lines. It happens, besides, that *Othello* is an extremely difficult play to cut. The cutter therefore, and not least an Elizabethan cutter to whom great poetry was, after all, no rarity, was bound to be ruthless with a passage which could be cut *en bloc* and with little sacrifice of *dramatic* effectiveness, which is his sole concern. There is in fact an effective bare abruptness in the passage as cut. I can see therefore no evidence at all that this passage was an addition. IV. i. 38-44; a not ineffective shortening of Othello's raving. IV. ii. 153-66; an unessential passage (ending, by the way, with an oddly Fletcherian line). IV. iii. 31-53 and 55-57; the song might no doubt be either cut or addition, except that the omission in V. ii. 253-55 looks unmistakably like a cut consequential on a cut here. IV. iii. 86-103; pretty clearly a cut of one of the very few passages of dramatic dead wood in the play. V. i. 82; this is the one passage which seems to me more probably an addition than a cut; it will be noticed that its absence from Q is connected with a difference of reading in l. 98, where Q (having only just mentioned it) reads *a chair*, whereas F reads *the chair*. V. ii. 192-200; a not impossible but certainly awkward cut. V. ii. 273-79; on the face of it an extremely clumsy cut; but I suggest that the transcriber or compositor blundered and that the cut should certainly have ended a line earlier and perhaps also begun a line earlier. To sum up, I can see no reason at all to suppose that any of these passages, with one doubtful and unimportant exception (which might have been made by any tinkerer), were later additions.

2. *Stage-directions*. The difference between Q and F is most striking. Put briefly, F, with I think four exceptions ('*pursuing Rodorigo*,' '*He falls in a trance*,' '*smothers her*' and '*dies*'), omits every one of the stage-directions which in Q illuminate the stage business and 'effects.' It omits, that is, the following: Brabantio's night gown in I. i., the table and lights in I. iii., the shot at II. i. 55, the trumpet and the kissing later in the same scene, '*Help, help*,' '*they fight*,' and the bell in II. iii. (apart from the fact that Roderigo is left without an exit at l. 129), both Othello's and Iago's kneeling in III. iii., and Cassio's essential withdrawal in

IV. i. 167, the trumpet in l. 209 of the same scene, Iago's light in V. i. and Othello's in V. ii. (though it gives Desdemona in her bed, which Q oddly does not), and, as will be observed on reference to the text, almost all the salient directions of this last scene; there are no directions for the deaths of either Desdemona or Emilia, nor for Othello's stabbing of himself, nor for Iago's murder of Emilia, and Cassio apparently enters upright on his feet. Taken by itself this difference in the stage-directions of course proves nothing as to the comparative authenticity of the two texts. Good stage-directions might no doubt accompany a poor text.

These are the facts: Q 1 retains the oaths, it makes various omissions, some of which are almost certainly dramatic cuts, and all of which (except some few which seem to have resulted from carelessness of compositor or transcriber) may be cuts, and its stage-directions are directions for the stage. These facts strongly suggest that with Q 1 we are in close contact with the play as Shakespeare wrote it and as it was played on the boards by his Majesty's servants between the time of its writing and 1606. My guess would be (though admittedly it is no more than a guess) that we are at a remove of no more than one transcript from the original MS.

It seems to me then that if we are to accept F as the superior and more authentic text, the text, that is, which brings us closer to Shakespeare, the *onus probandi* rests upon the supporters of the Folio; and I feel that the case has hardly been made out. But it is impossible to argue the case at all adequately within the limits of this preface, and in any case the final determination depends largely on the personal factor. I shall only attempt to give some general figures and to illustrate the kinds of difference which the two texts present. In the first place it may be noticed that even the 'Arden' editor, a whole-hearted supporter of F, feels himself driven to desert it 140 times in the course of the play (including some half-dozen preferences of Q 2 to either Q 1 or F). I think in fact that he might have stuck to his guns in some twenty of those instances, but in any event this means that any modern edition is going to prefer something over 100 readings of Q as against F. For myself, going to the other extreme, of just over 550 variants (leaving out of the count the presence or absence of oaths) noted in collating, I should regard 250 as being 'indifferent' (*i.e.* there seems nothing to choose between the two readings on grounds of sense, metre or vividness). And of the remaining 300 odd I should regard the reading of Q 1 as anything from 'slightly preferable' to 'definitely right' in 200 instances, that is in almost exactly double the number of instances where I should prefer F. This rough numerical way of stating the case is of course obviously unsatisfactory, since if the bulk of Q's preferred 200 readings belonged to the 'slightly preferable' class, whereas the bulk of F's 100 belonged to the 'clearly right' class, the mere numerical count would lose almost all its significance. It may perhaps be worth while to illustrate certain of the types of difference. (As in the numerical count I omit all consideration of the expurgated oaths, amusing though the study of them is, since the expurgator seems to have had a sort of sliding scale, so that where Q's language was moderately innocuous the oath disappears altogether, whereas when it was something more alarming like *Zounds* it is toned down to *Why*.) Nor need one waste time by observing the minor differences such as the reading of *does* for *doth*, or *you* for *ye*. In a number of cases F appears to be tidying up some minor awkwardness of rhythm (often by a mechanical counting of syllables), or regularising the grammar or idiom. In III. iii. 414 Q reads *Give me a*

living reason that she's disloyal; F omits *that*; or in IV. iii. 21, where
Q reads *Prithee unpin me—have grace and favour in them*, F omits the
in them, thereby reducing twelve syllables to the regulation ten,
but producing something which cannot be read as a line. Or in
III. i. 12 F reads *for love's sake* instead of Q's more colloquial *of all
loves*. Then there is a large class of differences of the 'singular-for-
plural' type (*thought* for *thoughts*, *part of his grief* for *part of his
griefs*, and so on) or such things as *Although 'tis fit* for *Though it be
fit*. Then there is the more important class where the difference
clearly depends on the misreading, at some stage of transcription
or printing, of the same original; such things as *Dawes* for *Doues*,
state for *senate*, *barke* for *bulke*. All these types of difference are
consonant with, and most of them indeed imply, the presence of a
common original behind both Q and F. There remains the much
smaller but much more puzzling class of differences which are not
referable to a common original. In I. iii. 252, for example, Q 1
reads *to the utmost pleasure of my lord*, whereas F reads *to the very
quality of my lord*; or in a famous passage, II. i. 63, Q 1 reads, *One
that excells the blasoning pens, And in the essentiall vesture of creation,
Does beare all excellency*; whereas F reads *One that excels the quirkes
of Blazoning pens, And in th' essentiall Vesture of Creation, Do's tyre
the Ingeniuer*. Clearly one of two things happened. Either the
transcriber of the copy for Q 1 or the compositor, having difficulty
with either the writing or the sense, filled in with something that
'would do,' or else F represents later emendations made by some
reviser in the original of Q 1. And it seems to me almost impossible to determine which of the two happened, or, if we accept
the second, who the reviser was. It will be noticed that in most
of the cases if we adhere to the *durior lectio* principle we are driven
to F's reading, and to the writing of long notes.

Finally, a word must be said about the Second Quarto. In its way it is perhaps the most interesting of all the Shakespearean texts, since it is demonstrably the result of a process of very careful editorial work. It is, to begin with, printed direct from a copy of Q 1. If one compares, for example, the passage I. iii. 312-33 in Q 1 and Q 2 one finds that Q 2 changes one comma to a question mark, inserts one comma, and reads two capital I's and one capital A for the corresponding lower-case letters; but that otherwise it corresponds with Q 1 not only word for word and letter for letter (with at least three noticeable spellings, *Ginny*, *Isop*, and *syen*), but also in the line-division. And this close similarity is observable throughout. It reproduces the stage-directions of Q 1, and also an unusual typographical feature of Q 1, the use of dots between phrases. But this copy of Q 1 had been most carefully collated either with F or with the MS. from which F was printed. Q 1's oaths are changed or omitted, but all the omitted passages are inserted. The collation is a very minute one, including again and again such small points as the alteration of Q 1's *ashore* to F's *on shore*. In the upshot Q 2 is an eclectic text. Of the 300 instances mentioned earlier, where one can express a preference as between Q 1 and F, Q 2 appears to select the preferable reading in 250 instances. Further, in about ten places Q 2 is not afraid to emend on its own account, almost always reasonably and for the better. From the standpoint of the determination of the text Q 2 has just this amount of importance. It is in no sense authoritative, since its editor cannot be proved, nor I think supposed, to have had access to any MS. But, for what it is worth, he clearly did not regard Q 1 as an inferior text, since in spite of the minuteness with which he corrects it by F he still adheres to it nearly twice as often as he deserts it. And when in the more critical divergences between Q 1 and F he adheres to Q 1 it means at least this, that a careful contemporary, who shows no reluctance at all to alter Q 1 when he sees cause, did not feel that in these instances any alteration was called for.

To sum up, I feel that with Q 1 we at least know where we are, while with F we do not. The text which follows is therefore based on Q 1. The omissions are restored; and where it is clear that a reading is the result of a transcriber's or compositor's explicable blunder the F reading is taken, often without comment. The passages peculiar to Q 1 are enclosed in square brackets, those peculiar to F in brace brackets. Q 1's typographical trick of dots is retained, since it clearly, I think, represents the original. Those stage-directions which are peculiar to the Quartos as against the Folio are also enclosed in square brackets, though a certain number of accepted directions which are in neither Quarto nor Folio are also admitted.

Date of Composition. The only direct evidence is a court performance of the play on November 1, 1604. We shall not be far out in accepting 1604 or late 1603 as the date of composition.

Source. The general outline of the story and many of the details are to be found in Giraldi Cinthio's *Ecatomiti* (1565). But as this was not, so far as we know, translated into English till more than two hundred years later, and as it does not contain any of Shakespeare's names except Desdemona, it is probable that there was some more immediate source, presumably a translation or adaptation of Cinthio now lost, something occupying the same position with regard to *Othello* that Whetstone's *Promos and Cassandra* occupies with regard to *Measure for Measure*.

Duration of Action. There has been great debate about this, and it is a plain enough fact that there are many passages in the play which are mutually inconsistent, some implying considerable intervals of time, others implying complete continuity of action during a comparatively brief time. If we look at the more obvious indications first, the progress seems to be clear. On the night of his marriage in Venice Othello is ordered to Cyprus and has only an hour with Desdemona before leaving. Desdemona sails for Cyprus after him but arrives before him. We can leave for the voyage any interval we choose; the extent of it has no relevance to the action of the play. At II. i. 182 Othello and Desdemona meet again in Cyprus. From this point there is hardly a break in the action; on this same day the herald announces the revelries for the evening; in the evening Cassio is made drunk and is cashiered; he announces his intention of enlisting Desdemona's aid 'betimes in the morning,' and follows this out at the beginning of Act III. Iago's insinuations begin, Desdemona drops the handkerchief, she and Othello go out to dinner, and Emilia gives the handkerchief to Iago, Othello re-enters and the temptation proceeds. There is just the possibility of an interval between III. iii. and III. iv., but I do not think it is natural to assume one longer than that necessary for Cassio to find the handkerchief. In this latter scene Cassio gives Bianca the handkerchief, and in IV. i. he has given it her 'even now.' Lodovico arrives from Venice and is bidden to supper. IV. ii. is 'at high supper time,' and Cassio is to be killed between twelve and one. The rest of the play, from IV. iii. to the end, happens just after this supper. That is to say that the whole of the action in Cyprus takes place, unless we insert an awkward interval in Act III., between about noon on Saturday and two or three a.m. on the Sunday-Monday night. And from certain points of view this rapid continuity of action is demanded by the situation. When once Iago's plot is launched it must succeed rapidly or it will never succeed at all; a chance meeting, for example, between Cassio and Othello would wreck it, and delay would so patently make it impossible that it would be dramatically absurd. But on the other side, from other points of view, this rapidity of action is no less absurd. To take only one point, Othello's interrogation of Emilia as to the relations between Cassio and Desdemona becomes quite meaningless. Emilia was only appointed to attend on Desdemona an hour before Othello, and, it is implied, Cassio, sailed from Venice, and Othello arrives in Cyprus within twenty minutes of Cassio. Further, on this time-scheme, it is bluntly impossible for the supposed adultery to have occurred; and even Othello's credulity cannot be supposed to swallow impossibilities. To give this side of the picture any sort of verisimilitude there must be supposed a reasonable period of time, either at Venice or Cyprus, during which Cassio and Desdemona might have conducted an intrigue. It has been argued that we must assume Othello's marriage to have happened some time before the opening of the play; but all the implications of Act I. are against this; and I have no doubt that the truth of the matter lies in the famous 'Double Time-scheme' theory, the theory, namely, that certain parts of the action are felt as behaving according to one time-scheme and others according to a much more leisurely time-scheme. This theory is sometimes attacked as though it implied that Shakespeare had worked with a kind of schedule in front of him, and said "now we are working by this clock and now by the other." I think that it was something much more instinctive than that, the skilled theatrical dramatist's knowledge of how far he can play on the natural reactions of his audience.

In fact any ordinary reader does not analyse the play by the clock; but he does 'feel' the play from one aspect moving fast and from another aspect moving slowly; or perhaps it would be more accurate to say that he feels, if one may put it so, the actual action moving fast, and the background of supposition against which it is set moving slowly. And Shakespeare knew that he could rely on his power of producing this very necessary illusion.

Criticism. Many critics and many readers would count this play the summit of Shakespeare's achievement, and so from the purely dramatic point of view it probably is. It is neither so profound as *Hamlet* nor so overwhelming as *Lear*. In general emotional impression it more nearly resembles *Macbeth*; it is superb theatre, and it is by far the most intense of all. There is none of that alternating increase and decrease of strain that is marked in the others. From the moment of the landing in Cyprus there is hardly a moment's relaxation of tension till the climax; and it is noteworthy that after Othello's death there is a far briefer quiet conclusion than in any of the others; only twelve lines. One is also, I think, more vividly aware of the operations of mere blind chance in this play than in any other tragedy of Shakespeare's except perhaps *Romeo and Juliet*. Even Iago's brilliance needs a deal of assistance from Fate to bring to a successful issue a plot whose extreme perils are only concealed from us by its success.

Rymer.[1]—Now (II. i. 100) follows a long ramble of Jack-pudden farce betwixt *Jago* and *Desdemona*, that runs on with all the little plays,

[1] *A Short View of Tragedy* (1693).

jingle, and trash below the patience of any Countrey Kitchin-maid with her Sweet-heart. The Venetian *Donna* is hard put to 't for pastime ! And this is all, when they are newly got on shoar, from a dismal Tempest, and when every moment she might expect to hear her Lord (as she calls him) that she runs so mad after, is arriv'd or lost. . . . Never in the World had any Pagan Poet his Brains turn'd at this Monstrous rate. But the ground of all this Bedlam-Buffoonry we saw, in the case of the French *Strolers*, the Company for Acting *Christ's Passion*, or the *Old Testament*, were Carpenters, Coblers, and illiterate fellows; who found that the Drolls, and Fooleries interlarded by them, brought in the rabble, and lengthened their time, so they got Money by the bargain. Our Shakespear, doubtless, was a great Master in this craft. These Carpenters and Coblers were the guides, he followed. And it is then no wonder that we find so much farce and *Apocryphal Matter* in his Tragedies. Thereby un-hallowing the Theatre, profaning the name of Tragedy; And instead of representing Men and Manners, turning all Morality, good sense, and humanity into mockery and derision. . . .

So much ado, so much stress, so much passion and repetition about a Handkerchief ! Why was not this call'd the *Tragedy of the Handkerchief* ? What can be more absurd than (as Quintilian expresses it) *in parvis litibus has Tragoedias movere* ? . . . Had it been *Desdemona's* Garter, the Sagacious Moor might have smelt a Rat : but the Handkerchief is so remote a trifle, no Booby, on this side *Mauritania*, cou'd make any consequence from it. . . .

What can remain with the Audience to carry home with them from this sort of Poetry, for their use and edification ? how can it work, unless (instead of settling the mind and purging our passions) to delude our senses, disorder our thoughts, addle our brain, pervert our affections, hair our imaginations, corrupt our appetite, and fill our head with vanity, confusion, *Tintamarre*, and Jingle-Jangle, beyond what all the Parish Clarks of *London*, with their *old Testament* farces, and interludes in *Richard* the seconds time, cou'd ever pretend to? Our only hopes, for the good of their souls, can be, that these people, go to the Playhouse, as they do to Church, to sit still, look one on another, make no reflection, nor mind the Play, more than they would a Sermon.

There is in this Play, some burlesk, some humour, and ramble of Comical Wit, some shew, and some *Mimickry* to divert the Spectator: but the Tragical part is, plainly none other, than a Bloody Farce, without salt or savour.

Johnson.—The beauties of this play impress themselves so strongly upon the attention of the reader, that they can draw no aid from critical illustration. The fiery openness of Othello, magnanimous, artless, and credulous, boundless in his confidence, ardent in his affection, inflexible in his resolution, and obdurate in his revenge; the cold malignity of Iago, silent in his resentment, subtle in his designs, and studious at once of his interest and his vengeance; the soft simplicity of Desdemona, confident of merit, and conscious of innocence, her artless perseverance in her suit, and her slowness to suspect that she can be suspected, are such proofs of Shakespeare's skill in human nature as, I suppose, it is vain to seek in any modern writer. The gradual progress which Iago makes in the Moor's conviction, and the circumstances which he employs to enflame him, are so artfully natural, that, though it will perhaps not be said of him as he says of himself, that he is 'a man not easily jealous,' yet we cannot but pity him, when at last we find him 'perplexed in the extreme.'

OTHELLO

Hazlitt.[1]—It has been said that tragedy purifies the affections by terror and pity. That is, it substitutes imaginary sympathy for mere selfishness. It gives us a high and permanent interest, beyond ourselves, in humanity as such. It raises the great, the remote, and the possible to an equality with the real, the little and the near. It makes man a partaker with his kind. It subdues and softens the stubbornness of his will. It teaches him that there are and have been others like himself, by shewing him as in a glass what they have felt, thought, and done. It opens the chambers of the human heart. It leaves nothing indifferent to us that can affect our common nature. It excites our sensibility by exhibiting the passions wound up to the utmost pitch by the power of imagination or the temptation of circumstances; and corrects their fatal excesses in ourselves by pointing to the greater extent of sufferings and of crimes to which they have led others. Tragedy creates a balance of the affections. It makes us thoughtful spectators in the lists of life. It is the refiner of the species; a discipline of humanity. The habitual study of poetry and works of imagination is one chief part of a well-grounded education. A taste for liberal art is necessary to complete the character of a gentleman. Science alone is hard and mechanical. It exercises the understanding upon things out of ourselves, while it leaves the affections unemployed, or engrossed with our own immediate, narrow interests. OTHELLO furnishes an illustration of these remarks. It excites our sympathy in an extraordinary degree. The moral it conveys has a closer application to the concerns of human life than that of any other of Shakespear's plays. 'It comes directly home to the bosoms and business of men.' The pathos in *Lear* is indeed more dreadful and overpowering: but it is less natural,

---

[1] Hazlitt. *Characters of Shakespear's Plays.*

and less of every day's occurrence. We have not the same degree of sympathy with the passions described in *Macbeth*. The interest in *Hamlet* is more remote and reflex. That of *Othello* is at once equally profound and affecting.

. . . The third act of OTHELLO is his master-piece, not of knowledge or passion separately, but of the two combined, of the knowledge of character with the expression of passion, of consummate art in the keeping up of appearances with the profound workings of nature, and the convulsive movements of uncontroulable agony, of the power of inflicting torture and of suffering it. . . . Iago in fact belongs to a class of characters, common to Shakespear and at the same time peculiar to him; whose heads are as acute and active as their hearts are hard and callous. Iago is to be sure an extreme instance of the kind; that is to say, of diseased intellectual activity, with an almost perfect indifference to moral good or evil, or rather with a decided preference of the latter, because it falls more readily in with his favourite propensity, gives greater zest to his thoughts and scope to his actions. He is quite or nearly as indifferent to his own fate as to that of others; he runs all risks for a trifling and doubtful advantage; and is himself the dupe and victim of his ruling passion—an insatiable craving after action of the most difficult and dangerous kind.

Swinburne.[1]—As surely as Othello is the noblest man of man's making, Iago is the most perfect evil-doer, the most potent demi-devil. . . . Malignant as he is, the very subtlest and strongest component of his complex nature is not even malignity. It is the instinct of what Mr Carlyle would call an inarticulate poet. . . . With all his poetic gift, he has no poetic weakness. Almost any

[1] Swinburne. *A Study of Shakespeare.*

creator but his would have given him some grain of spite or some spark of lust after Desdemona. To Shakespeare's Iago she is no more than is a rhyme to another and articulate poet. . . . He has within him a sense or conscience of power incomparable: and this power shall not be left, in Hamlet's phrase, 'to fust in him unused.' A genuine and thorough capacity for human lust or hate would diminish and degrade the supremacy of his evil. He is almost as far above or beyond vice as he is beneath or beyond virtue. And this it is that makes him impregnable and invulnerable.

Bradley.—What is the peculiarity of *Othello*? What is the distinctive impression that it leaves? Of all Shakespeare's tragedies, I would answer, not even excepting *King Lear*, *Othello* is the most painfully exciting and the most terrible. From the moment when the temptation of the hero begins, the reader's heart and mind are held in a vice, experiencing the extremes of pity and fear, sympathy and repulsion, sickening hope and dreadful expectation. Evil is displayed before him, not indeed with the profusion found in *King Lear*, but forming, as it were, the soul of a single character, and united with an intellectual superiority so great that he watches its advance fascinated and appalled. He sees it, in itself almost irresistible, aided at every step by fortunate accidents and the innocent mistakes of its victims. He seems to breathe an atmosphere as fateful as that of *King Lear*, but more confined and oppressive, the darkness not of night but of a close-shut murderous room. His imagination is excited to intense activity, but it is the activity of concentration rather than dilation.

OTHELLO, THE MOOR OF VENICE

DRAMATIS PERSONÆ

DUKE OF VENICE.

BRABANTIO, *a senator.*

Other Senators.

GRATIANO, *brother to Brabantio.*

LODOVICO, *kinsman to Brabantio.*

OTHELLO, *a noble Moor in the service of the Venetian state.*

CASSIO, *his lieutenant.*

IAGO, *his ancient.*

RODERIGO, *a Venetian gentleman.*

MONTANO, *Othello's predecessor in the government of Cyprus.*

Clown, *servant to Othello.*

DESDEMONA, *daughter to Brabantio and wife to Othello.*

EMILIA, *wife to Iago.*

BIANCA, *mistress to Cassio.*

Sailor, Messenger, Herald, Officers, Gentlemen, Musicians, and Attendants.

SCENE: *Venice ; a seaport in Cyprus.*

THE TRAGEDY OF OTHELLO
THE MOOR OF VENICE

Act First

SCENE I

Venice. A street

Enter Roderigo and Iago

Rod. Tush, never tell me, I take it much unkindly
    That you, Iago, who has had my purse,
    As if the strings were thine, shouldst know of this.

Iago. 'Sblood, but you will not hear me :
    If ever I did dream of such a matter,
    Abhor me.

Rod. Thou told'st me thou didst hold him in thy hate.

Iago. Despise me if I do not : three great ones of the city,
    In personal suit to make me his lieutenant,
    Oft capp'd to him : and, by the faith of man,   10
    I know my price, I am worth no worse a place.
    But he, as loving his own pride and purposes,
    Evades them, with a bombast circumstance
    Horribly stuff'd with epithets of war ;

[And, in conclusion,]
Nonsuits my mediators; for, 'Certes,' says he,
'I have already chosen my officer.'
And what was he?
Forsooth, a great arithmetician,
One Michael Cassio, a Florentine,   20
A fellow almost damn'd in a fair wife;   †
That never set a squadron in the field,
Nor the division of a battle knows
More than a spinster, unless the bookish theoric,
Wherein the toged consuls can propose
As masterly as he: mere prattle without practice
Is all his soldiership: but he, sir, had the election,
And I, of whom his eyes had seen the proof,
At Rhodes, at Cyprus, and on other grounds,
Christian and heathen, must be be-lee'd and calm'd †
By debitor and creditor: this counter-caster,   31
He, in good time, must his lieutenant be,
And I—God bless the mark!—his worship's ancient. †

Rod. By heaven, I rather would have been his hangman.

Iago. But there's no remedy, 'tis the curse of service,
Preferment goes by letter and affection,
Not by the old gradation, where each second
Stood heir to the first. Now, sir, be judge yourself
Whether I in any just term am affin'd

To love the Moor.

Rod.   I would not follow him then.   40

Iago. O sir, content you ;

I follow him to serve my turn upon him :

We cannot all be masters, nor all masters

Cannot be truly follow'd.   You shall mark

Many a duteous and knee-crooking knave,

That doting on his own obsequious bondage

Wears out his time much like his master's ass,

For nought but provender, and when he 's old, cashier'd :

Whip me such honest knaves.   Others there are

Who, trimm'd in forms and visages of duty,   50

Keep yet their hearts attending on themselves,

And throwing but shows of service on their lords

Do well thrive by 'em, and when they have lin'd their
     coats

Do themselves homage : those fellows have some soul,

And such a one do I profess myself, . . . for, sir,

It is as sure as you are Roderigo,

Were I the Moor, I would not be Iago :

In following him, I follow but myself ;

Heaven is my judge, not I for love and duty,

But seeming so, for my peculiar end :   60

For when my outward action does demonstrate

The native act and figure of my heart

In complement extern, 'tis not long after
But I will wear my heart upon my sleeve
For daws to peck at : I am not what I am.

Rod. What a full fortune does the thick-lips owe,
If he can carry 't thus !

Iago.   Call up her father,
Rouse him, make after him, poison his delight,
Proclaim him in the streets, incense her kinsmen,
And, though he in a fertile climate dwell,   70
Plague him with flies : though that his joy be joy,
Yet throw such changes of vexation on 't
As it may lose some colour.

Rod. Here is her father's house, I'll call aloud.

Iago. Do, with like timorous accent, and dire yell,
As when, by night and negligence, the fire
Is spied in populous cities.

Rod. What, ho, Brabantio !   Signior Brabantio, ho !

Iago. Awake ! what, ho, Brabantio ! thieves ! thieves !
     [thieves !]
Look to your house, your daughter and your bags !   80
Thieves ! thieves !

     Brabantio appears above, at a window

Bra. What is the reason of this terrible summons ?
What is the matter there ?

Rod. Signior, is all your family within ?

Iago. Are all doors lock'd ?

Bra.   Why, wherefore ask you this ?

Iago. 'Zounds, sir, you 're robb'd ; for shame, put on your
       gown ;

     Your heart is burst, you have lost half your soul ;

     Even now, now, very now, an old black ram

     Is tupping your white ewe ; arise, arise,

     Awake the snorting citizens with the bell,   90

     Or else the devil will make a grandsire of you :

     Arise, I say.

Bra.   What, have you lost your wits ?

Rod. Most reverend signior, do you know my voice ?

Bra. Not I, what are you ?

Rod. My name is Roderigo.

Bra.   The worse welcome :

     I have charg'd thee not to haunt about my doors,

     In honest plainness thou hast heard me say

     My daughter is not for thee, and now, in madness,

     Being full of supper, and distempering draughts,

     Upon malicious bravery, dost thou come   100

     To start my quiet ?

Rod. Sir, sir, sir,—

Bra.   But thou must needs be sure

     My spirit and my place have in them power

     To make this bitter to thee.

Rod.   Patience, good sir.

Bra. What tell'st thou me of robbing? this is Venice,
My house is not a grange.

Rod.   Most grave Brabantio,
In simple and pure soul I come to you.

Iago. 'Zounds, sir, you are one of those that will not
serve God, if the devil bid you.   Because we come
to do you service, you think we are ruffians; you 'll 110
have your daughter covered with a Barbary horse;
you 'll have your nephews neigh to you; you 'll
have coursers for cousins, and gennets for germans.

Bra. What profane wretch art thou?

Iago. I am one, sir, that come to tell you, your daughter,
and the Moor, are now making the beast with two
backs.

Bra. Thou art a villain.

Iago.   You are a senator.

Bra. This thou shalt answer, I know thee, Roderigo.

Rod. Sir, I will answer any thing.   But, I beseech you,   120
{If 't be your pleasure and most wise consent,
(As partly I find it is) that your fair daughter,
At this odd-even and dull watch o' the night,
Transported with no worse nor better guard
But with a knave of common hire, a gondolier,
To the gross clasps of a lascivious Moor,—

6

If this be known to you, and your allowance,
We then have done you bold and saucy wrongs ;
But if you know not this, my manners tell me
We have your wrong rebuke.   Do not believe   130
That, from the sense of all civility,
I thus would play and trifle with your reverence :
Your daughter (if you have not given her leave)
I say again, hath made a gross revolt,
Tying her duty, beauty, wit and fortunes,
In an extravagant and wheeling stranger
Of here, and every where.   Straight satisfy yourself.}
If she be in her chamber, or your house,
Let loose on me the justice of the state
For this delusion.

Bra.   Strike on the tinder, ho !   140
Give me a taper, call up all my people !
This accident is not unlike my dream,
Belief of it oppresses me already.

Light, I say, light !   *Exit above*

Iago.   Farewell, for I must leave you ;
It seems not meet, nor wholesome to my place,
To be produc'd, as if I stay I shall,
Against the Moor, for I do know the state,
However this may gall him with some check,
Cannot with safety cast him ; for he's embark'd,

With such loud reason, to the Cyprus wars,   150
Which even now stands in act, that, for their souls,
Another of his fathom they have not
To lead their business ; in which regard,
Though I do hate him, as I do hell's pains,
Yet for necessity of present life,
I must show out a flag and sign of love,
Which is indeed but sign.   That you shall surely find
      him,
Lead to the Sagittary the raised search ;   †
And there will I be with him.   So farewell.   *Exit*
Enter, below, Brabantio, [in his night-gown,] and Servants
*   with torches*

Bra. It is too true an evil, gone she is,   160
And what's to come, of my despised time,
Is nought but bitterness.   Now, Roderigo,
Where didst thou see her ?   O unhappy girl,
With the Moor, say'st thou ?   Who would be a
      father ?
How didst thou know 'twas she ?   O, thou deceiv'st
      me
Past thought !   What said she to you ?   Get more
      tapers,
Raise all my kindred, are they married, think you ?
Rod. Truly, I think they are.

8

Bra. O heaven ! How got she out ? O treason of the
      blood !
  Fathers, from hence trust not your daughters' minds, 170
  By what you see them act, is there not charms,
  By which the property of youth and maidhood
  May be abus'd ? Have you not read, Roderigo,
  Of some such thing ?

Rod.   I have, sir.

Bra. Call up my brother. O that you had had her !
  Some one way, some another ; do you know
  Where we may apprehend her, and the Moor ?

Rod. I think I can discover him, if you please
  To get good guard, and go along with me.

Bra. Pray you, lead on ; at every house I'll call,   180
  I may command at most. Get weapons, ho !
  And raise some special officers of night :   †
  On, good Roderigo, I'll deserve your pains.   *Exeunt*

SCENE II

Another street

Enter Othello, Iago, and Attendants with torches

Iago. Though in the trade of war I have slain men,
  Yet do I hold it very stuff o' the conscience

9

     To do no contriv'd murder : I lack iniquity
     Sometimes to do me service : nine or ten times
     I had thought to have yerk'd him here under the ribs.

Oth. 'Tis better as it is.

Iago.   Nay, but he prated
     And spoke such scurvy and provoking terms
     Against your honour,
     That, with the little godliness I have,
     I did full hard forbear him. But I pray, sir,   10
     Are you fast married ? For be sure of this,
     That the magnifico is much belov'd,
     And hath in his effect a voice potential
     As double as the duke's ; he will divorce you,
     Or put upon you what restraint and grievance
     The law, with all his might to enforce it on,
     Will give him cable.

Oth.   Let him do his spite :
     My services, which I have done the signiory,
     Shall out-tongue his complaints. 'Tis yet to know—
     {Which, when I know} that boasting is an honour,   20
     I shall provulgate—I fetch my life and being
     From men of royal siege, and my demerits   †
     May speak unbonneted to as proud a fortune
     As this that I have reach'd ; for know, Iago,
     But that I love the gentle Desdemona,

I would not my unhoused free condition
Put into circumscription and confine
For the sea's worth.   But, look ! what lights come
    yonder ?

Iago. These are the raised father and his friends,
You were best go in.

Oth.   Not I, I must be found :   30
My parts, my title, and my perfect soul,
Shall manifest me rightly.   Is it they ?

Iago. By Janus, I think no.

     Enter Cassio, and certain Officers with torches

Oth. The servants of the duke, and my lieutenant.
The goodness of the night upon you, friends !
What is the news ?

Cas.   The duke does greet you, general,
And he requires your haste-post-haste appearance,
Even on the instant.

Oth.   What's the matter, think you ?

Cas. Something from Cyprus, as I may divine ;
It is a business of some heat, the galleys   40
Have sent a dozen sequent messengers
This very night, at one another's heels ;
And many of the consuls, rais'd and met,
Are at the duke's already : you have been hotly
    call'd for,

When, being not at your lodging to be found,
The senate sent about three several quests
To search you out.

Oth. 'Tis well I am found by you.
I will but spend a word here in the house,
And go with you. *Exit*

Cas. Ancient, what makes he here?

Iago. Faith, he to-night hath boarded a land carack: 50
If it prove lawful prize, he's made for ever.

Cas. I do not understand.

Iago. He's married.

Cas. To who?

Re-enter Othello

Iago. Marry, to—Come, captain, will you go?

Oth. Ha' with you.

Cas. Here comes another troop to seek for you.

Iago. It is Brabantio; general, be advis'd,
He comes to bad intent.

*Enter Brabantio, Roderigo, and others with lights and
weapons*

Oth. Holla! stand there!

Rod. Signior, it is the Moor.

Bra. Down with him, thief!

They draw on both sides

Iago. You, Roderigo, come, sir, I am for you.

Oth. Keep up your bright swords, for the dew will rust 'em ;
　　Good signior, you shall more command with years　　60
　　Than with your weapons.

Bra. O thou foul thief, where hast thou stow'd my daughter ?
　　Damn'd as thou art, thou hast enchanted her ;
　　For I'll refer me to all things of sense,
　　{If she in chains of magic were not bound,}
　　Whether a maid so tender, fair, and happy,
　　So opposite to marriage that she shunn'd
　　The wealthy curled darlings of our nation,
　　Would ever have (to incur a general mock)
　　Run from her guardage to the sooty bosom　　70
　　Of such a thing as thou ? to fear, not to delight :
　　{Judge me the world, if 'tis not gross in sense
　　That thou hast practis'd on her with foul charms,
　　Abus'd her delicate youth, with drugs or minerals
　　That weaken motion : I'll have 't disputed on ;
　　'Tis probable, and palpable to thinking.
　　I therefore apprehend and do attach thee
　　For} an abuser of the world, a practiser　　†
　　Of arts inhibited, and out of warrant.
　　Lay hold upon him : if he do resist,　　80
　　Subdue him at his peril.

Oth.　　　　　　　　　　Hold your hands ;
　　Both you of my inclining and the rest :

13

Were it my cue to fight, I should have known it
Without a prompter ; where will you that I go,
To answer this your charge ?

Bra.   To prison, till fit time
Of law, and course of direct session
Call thee to answer.

Oth.   What if I do obey ?
How may the duke be therewith satisfied,
Whose messengers are here about my side,
Upon some present business of the state   9c
To bear me to him ?

1.O.   'Tis true, most worthy signior ;
The duke's in council, and your noble self,
I am sure, is sent for.

Bra.   How ? the duke in council ?
In this time of the night ?   Bring him away,
Mine's not an idle cause, the duke himself,
Or any of my brothers of the state,
Cannot but feel this wrong as 'twere their own.
For if such actions may have passage free,
Bond-slaves, and pagans, shall our statesmen be.

            Exeunt

SCENE III

A council-chamber

*The Duke and Senators [sitting at a table with lights] and
Attendants*

Du. There is no composition in these news
       That gives them credit.

1.S.   Indeed they are disproportion'd;
       My letters say, a hundred and seven galleys.

Du. And mine, a hundred and forty.

2.S.   And mine, two hundred:
       But though they jump not on a just account,—
       As in these cases, where they aim reports,
       'Tis oft with difference,—yet do they all confirm
       A Turkish fleet, and bearing up to Cyprus.

Du. Nay, it is possible enough to judgement:
       I do not so secure me to the error,   10
       But the main article I do approve
       In fearful sense.

Sail.   (*within*) What, ho! what, ho! what, ho!

1.O. A messenger from the galleys.

Enter Sailor

Du.   Now, the business?

Sail. The Turkish preparation makes for Rhodes;

So was I bid report here to the state.
{By Signior Angelo.}
Du. How say you by this change?
1.*S.* This cannot be by no assay of reason . . .
'Tis a pageant,
To keep us in false gaze: when we consider   20
The importancy of Cyprus to the Turk,
And let ourselves again but understand
That as it more concerns the Turk than Rhodes,
So may he with more facile question bear it,
{For that it stands not in such warlike brace,
But altogether lacks the abilities
That Rhodes is dress'd in: if we make thought of this,
We must not think the Turk is so unskilful
To leave that latest which concerns him first,
Neglecting an attempt of ease, and gain,   30
To wake and wage a danger profitless.}
Du. Nay, in all confidence, he's not for Rhodes.
1.*O.* Here is more news.

            Enter a Messenger

Mes. The Ottomites, reverend and gracious,
Steering with due course toward the isle of Rhodes,
Have there injointed with an after fleet.
{1.*S.*Ay, so I thought. How many, as you guess?
Mes.}Of thirty sail, and now they do re-stem

Their backward course, bearing with frank appearance
Their purposes towards Cyprus.   Signior Montano,   40
Your trusty and most valiant servitor,
With his free duty recommends you thus,
And prays you to believe him.

Du. 'Tis certain then for Cyprus.
　　Marcus Luccicos is not here in town.

1.S. He's now in Florence.

Du. Write from us, wish him post-post-haste dispatch.

1.S. Here comes Brabantio and the valiant Moor.

　　　Enter Brabantio, Othello, Iago, Roderigo, Cassio,
　　　　　　　and Officers

Du. Valiant Othello, we must straight employ you,
　　Against the general enemy Ottoman.   50
　　(*to Bra.*) I did not see you, welcome, gentle signior ;
　　We lack'd your counsel and your help to-night.

Bra. So did I yours ; good your grace, pardon me,
　　Neither my place, nor aught I heard of business,
　　Hath rais'd me from my bed, nor doth the general care
　　Take any hold of me ; for my particular grief
　　Is of so flood-gate and o'erbearing nature
　　That is engluts and swallows other sorrows,
　　And it is still itself.

Du. 　　　　　　Why, what's the matter ?

Bra. My daughter, O, my daughter !

17

All.   Dead ?

Bra.   Ay, to me ;   60
    She is abus'd, stol'n from me and corrupted
    By spells and medicines, bought of mountebanks,
    For nature so preposterously to err,
    {Being not deficient, blind, or lame of sense,}
    Sans witchcraft could not.

Du. Whoe'er he be that in this foul proceeding
    Hath thus beguil'd your daughter of herself,
    And you of her, the bloody book of law
    You shall yourself read in the bitter letter,
    After its own sense, though our proper son   70
    Stood in your action.

Bra.   Humbly I thank your grace ;
    Here is the man, this Moor, whom now, it seems,
    Your special mandate for the state-affairs
    Hath hither brought.

All.   We are very sorry for 't.

Du. (*to Oth.*) What in your own part can you say to this ?

Bra. Nothing, but this is so.

Oth. Most potent, grave, and reverend signiors,
    My very noble and approv'd good masters :
    That I have ta'en away this old man's daughter,
    It is most true ; true, I have married her ;   80
    The very head and front of my offending

Hath this extent, no more.   Rude am I in my speech,
And little blest with the set phrase of peace ;   †
For since these arms of mine had seven years' pith,
Till now some nine moons wasted, they have us'd
Their dearest action in the tented field,
And little of this great world can I speak,
More than pertains to feats of broil and battle :
And therefore little shall I grace my cause
In speaking for myself ; yet, by your gracious patience,
I will a round unvarnish'd tale deliver   91
Of my whole course of love, what drugs, what charms,
What conjuration, and what mighty magic
(For such proceedings am I charg'd withal)
I won his daughter.

Bra.   A maiden never bold ;
Of spirit so still and quiet that her motion
Blush'd at herself ; and she in spite of nature,
Of years, of country, credit, every thing,
To fall in love with what she fear'd to look on ?
It is a judgement maim'd, and most imperfect,   100
That will confess perfection so could err
Against all rules of nature, and must be driven
To find out practices of cunning hell,
Why this should be ; I therefore vouch again,
That with some mixtures powerful o'er the blood,

Or with some dram conjur'd to this effect,
He wrought upon her.

Du.   To vouch this is no proof,
Without more certain and more overt test ;
These art thin habits, and poor likelihoods,
Of modern seemings, you prefer against him.   110

1.S. But Othello, speak :
Did you by indirect and forced courses
Subdue and poison this young maid's affections ?
Or came it by request, and such fair question
As soul to soul affordeth ?

Oth.   I do beseech you,
Send for the lady to the Sagittary,
And let her speak of me before her father ;
If you do find me foul in her report,
{The trust, the office I do hold of you,}
Not only take away, but let your sentence   120
Even fall upon my life.

Du.   Fetch Desdemona hither.

                        Exit two or three

Oth. Ancient, conduct them, you best know the place.

                            Exit Iago

And till she come, as truly as to heaven
{I do confess the vices of my blood,}
So justly to your grave ears I'll present

How I did thrive in this fair lady's love,
And she in mine.

Du. Say it, Othello.

Oth. Her father lov'd me, oft invited me,
Still question'd me the story of my life,   130
From year to year ; the battles, sieges, fortunes,
That I have pass'd :
I ran it through, even from my boyish days
To the very moment that he bade me tell it :
Wherein I spake of most disastrous chances,
Of moving accidents by flood and field ;
Of hair-breadth 'scapes i' the imminent deadly
    breach ;
Of being taken by the insolent foe ;
And sold to slavery, and my redemption thence,
And with it all my travels' history :   140
Wherein of antres vast, and deserts idle,
Rough quarries, rocks and hills, whose heads touch
    heaven,
It was my hint to speak,—such was the process ;
And of the Cannibals, that each other eat,
The Anthropophagi ; and men whose heads
Do grow beneath their shoulders : this to hear
Would Desdemona seriously incline ;
But still the house-affairs would draw her thence,

Which ever as she could with haste dispatch,
She'ld come again, and with a greedy ear   150
Devour up my discourse ; which I observing,
Took once a pliant hour, and found good means
To draw from her a prayer of earnest heart
That I would all my pilgrimage dilate,
Whereof by parcel she had something heard,
But not intentively : I did consent,
And often did beguile her of her tears,   †
When I did speak of some distressful stroke
That my youth suffer'd : my story being done,
She gave me for my pains a world of sighs :   160
She swore, i' faith, 'twas strange, 'twas passing
        strange ;
'Twas pitiful, 'twas wondrous pitiful ;
She wish'd she had not heard it, yet she wish'd
That heaven had made her such a man : she thank'd
        me,
And bade me, if I had a friend that lov'd her,
I should but teach him how to tell my story,
And that would woo her.   Upon this hint I spake :
She lov'd me for the dangers I had pass'd,
And I lov'd her that she did pity them.
This only is the witchcraft I have us'd.   170
Here comes the lady, let her witness it.

Enter Desdemona, Iago, and Attendants

Du. I think this tale would win my daughter too . . .
  Good Brabantio,
  Take up this mangled matter at the best :
  Men do their broken weapons rather use
  Than their bare hands.

Bra.   I pray you hear her speak.
  If she confess that she was half the wooer,
  Destruction light on me, if my bad blame
  Light on the man !   Come hither, gentle mistress :
  Do you perceive in all this noble company   180
  Where most you owe obedience ?

Des.   My noble father,
  I do perceive here a divided duty :
  To you I am bound for life and education ;
  My life and education both do learn me
  How to respect you ; you 're lord of all my duty,
  I am hitherto your daughter : but here 's my husband,
  And so much duty as my mother show'd
  To you, preferring you before her father,
  So much I challenge that I may profess
  Due to the Moor my lord.

Bra.   God bu'y, I ha' done.   190
  Please it your grace, on to the state-affairs :
  I had rather to adopt a child than get it.

Come hither, Moor :
I here do give thee that, with all my heart
{Which, but thou hast already, with all my heart} †
I would keep from thee.   For your sake, jewel,
I am glad at soul I have no other child ;
For thy escape would teach me tyranny,
To hang clogs on 'em ; I have done, my lord.

Du. Let me speak like yourself, and lay a sentence   200
Which, as a greese or step, may help these lovers
[Into your favour.]
When remedies are past, the griefs are ended,
By seeing the worst, which late on hopes depended.
To mourn a mischief that is past and gone
Is the next way to draw more mischief on ;
What cannot be preserv'd when fortune takes,
Patience her injury a mockery makes.
The robb'd that smiles steals something from the
    thief ;
He robs himself that spends a bootless grief.   210

Bra. So let the Turk of Cyprus us beguile,
We lose it not so long as we can smile ;
He bears the sentence well, that nothing bears
But the free comfort, which from thence he hears ;
But he bears both the sentence and the sorrow,
That, to pay grief, must of poor patience borrow

These sentences, to sugar or to gall,
Being strong on both sides, are equivocal:
But words are words; I never yet did hear
That the bruis'd heart was pierced through the ear. 220
Beseech you now, to the affairs of state.

Du. The Turk with most mighty preparation makes for
Cyprus: Othello, the fortitude of the place is best
known to you, and though we have there a substitute
of most allowed sufficiency, yet opinion, a sovereign
mistress of effects, throws a more safer voice on
you: you must therefore be content to slubber the
gloss of your new fortunes with this more stubborn
and boisterous expedition.

Oth. The tyrant custom, most grave senators, 230
Hath made the flinty and steel couch of war
My thrice-driven bed of down: I do agnize
A natural and prompt alacrity
I find in hardness, and do undertake
These present wars against the Ottomites.
Most humbly therefore, bending to your state,
I crave fit disposition for my wife,
Due reverence of place and exhibition,
With such accommodation and besort
As levels with her breeding.

Du.   If you please, 240

    Be't at her father's.

Bra.   I'll not have it so.

Oth. Nor I.

Des.   Nor I, I would not there reside,
    To put my father in impatient thoughts
    By being in his eye : most gracious duke.
    To my unfolding lend a gracious ear,
    And let me find a charter in your voice
    And if my simpleness . . .

Du. What would you . . . speak.

Des. That I did love the Moor, to live with him,
    My downright violence, and scorn of fortunes,   †
    May trumpet to the world : my heart's subdued   251
    Even to the utmost pleasure of my lord :
    I saw Othello's visage in his mind,
    And to his honours and his valiant parts
    Did I my soul and fortunes consecrate :
    So that, dear lords, if I be left behind,
    A moth of peace, and he go to the war,
    The rites for which I love him are bereft me.
    And I a heavy interim shall support
    By his dear absence ; let me go with him.   260

Oth. Your voices, Lords ! Beseech you, let her will
    Have a free way : I therefore beg it not,
    To please the palate of my appetite ;

Nor to comply with heat, the young affects †
In my defunct and proper satisfaction,
But to be free and bounteous of her mind ;
And heaven defend your good souls that you think
I will your serious and great business scant
For she is with me ; . . . no, when light-wing'd toys
And feather'd Cupid foils with wanton dullness ‡
My speculative and active instruments, 271
That my disports corrupt and taint my business,
Let housewives make a skillet of my helm,
And all indign and base adversities
Make head against my reputation !

Du. Be it as you shall privately determine,
Either for stay or going : the affair cries haste,
And speed must answer 't ; you must hence to-night.

[*Des.*To-night, my lord ?

Du.   This night.]

Oth.   With all my heart.

Du. At ten i' the morning here we 'll meet again. 280
Othello, leave some officer behind,
And he shall our commission bring to you,
With such things else of quality or respect
As doth concern you.

Oth.   Please your grace, my ancient ;
A man he is of honesty and trust :

To his conveyance I assign my wife,
With what else needful your good grace shall think
To be sent after me.

Du.   Let it be so.

Good night to every one. *(to Bra.)* And, noble
     signior,
If virtue no delighted beauty lack,   290
Your son-in-law is far more fair than black.

1.S. Adieu, brave Moor, use Desdemona well.

Bra. Look to her, Moor, have a quick eye to see :
She has deceiv'd her father, may do thee.

           Exeunt Duke, Senators, Officers. &c.

Oth. My life upon her faith ! Honest Iago,
My Desdemona must I leave to thee :
I prithee, let thy wife attend on her,
And bring her after in the best advantage.
Come, Desdemona, I have but an hour
Of love, of worldly matters, and direction,   300
To spend with thee : we must obey the time.

           Exeunt Othello and Desdemona

Rod. Iago !

Iago. What say'st thou, noble heart ?

Rod. What will I do, thinkest thou ?

Iago. Why, go to bed and sleep.

Rod. I will incontinently drown myself.

Iago. If thou dost, I shall never love thee after it.
    Why, thou silly gentleman ?

Rod. It is silliness to live when to live is a torment, and
    then we have a prescription to die, when death is 310
    our physician.

Iago. {O villanous !}   I have look'd upon the world for
    four times seven years, and since I could distinguish
    between a benefit and an injury, I never found man
    that knew how to love himself : ere I would say I
    would drown myself for the love of a guinea-hen,
    I would change my humanity with a baboon.

Rod. What should I do ?   I confess it is my shame to be
    so fond, but it is not in my virtue to amend it.

Iago. Virtue ? a fig ! 'tis in ourselves that we are thus, or 320
    thus ; our bodies are gardens, to the which our wills
    are gardeners, so that if we will plant nettles, or sow
    lettuce, set hyssop, and weed up thyme ; supply it
    with one gender of herbs, or distract it with many ;
    either to have it sterile with idleness, or manur'd with
    industry, why, the power, and corrigible authority
    of this, lies in our wills.   If the balance of our lives
    had not one scale of reason to poise another of
    sensuality, the blood and baseness of our natures
    would conduct us to most preposterous conclusions : 330
    but we have reason to cool our raging motions, our

carnal stings, our unbitted lusts; whereof I take
this, that you call love, to be a sect or scion.

Rod. It cannot be.

Iago. It is merely a lust of the blood, and a permission of
the will. Come, be a man : drown thyself ? drown
cats and blind puppies. I profess me thy friend,
and I confess me knit to thy deserving, with cables
of perdurable toughness : I could never better
stead thee than now. Put money in thy purse ; 340
follow these wars, defeat thy favour with an usurp'd
beard ; I say, put money in thy purse. It cannot
be that Desdemona should long continue her love
unto the Moor . . . put money in thy purse . . .
nor he to her : it was a violent commencement, and
thou shalt see an answerable sequestration ; put but
money in thy purse. . . . These Moors are change-
able in their wills : . . . fill thy purse with money.
The food that to him now is as luscious as locusts,
shall be to him shortly as acerb as the coloquintida. †
{She must change for youth :} when she is sated 351
with his body, she will find the error of her choice :
[she must have change, she must.] Therefore put
money in thy purse : if thou wilt needs damn thyself, do it a more delicate way than drowning,
make all the money thou canst. If sanctimony, and

a frail vow, betwixt an erring barbarian, and a super-
subtle Venetian, be not too hard for my wits, and
all the tribe of hell, thou shalt enjoy her; therefore
make money, . . . a pox of drowning thyself! 360
'tis clean out of the way: seek thou rather to be
hang'd, in compassing thy joy, than to be drowned,
and go without her.

Rod. Wilt thou be fast to my hopes{, if I depend on the
issue} ?

Iago. Thou art sure of me . . . go, make money. . . . I
have told thee often, and I tell thee again, and
again, I hate the Moor; my cause is hearted, thine
has no less reason, let us be conjunctive in our
revenge against him: if thou canst cuckold him, 370
thou doest thyself a pleasure, and me a sport.   There
are many events in the womb of time, which will be
delivered.   Traverse, go, provide thy money, we
will have more of this to-morrow.   Adieu.

Rod. Where shall we meet i' the morning ?

Iago. At my lodging.

Rod. I 'll be with thee betimes.

Iago, Go to, farewell : . . . do you hear, Roderigo ?

Rod. [What say you ?

Iago. No more of drowning, do you hear ? 380

Rod. I am chang'd :] {I 'll go sell all my land.}   *Exit*

Iago. Go to, farewell, put money enough in your purse !]
Thus do I ever make my fool my purse ;
For I mine own gain'd knowledge should profane,
If I would time expend with such a snipe
But for my sport and profit.   I hate the Moor,
And it is thought abroad that 'twixt my sheets
He's done my office ; I know not if 't be true . . .
Yet I, for mere suspicion in that kind,
Will do, as if for surety : he holds me well ;   390
The better shall my purpose work on him.
Cassio's a proper man : let me see now ;
To get his place, and to make up my will,   †
A double knavery. . . . How, how ? . . . Let me see :
After some time, to abuse Othello's ear
That he is too familiar with his wife :
He hath a person and a smooth dispose
To be suspected, fram'd to make women false :
The Moor a free and open nature too,
That thinks men honest that but seem to be so ;   400
And will as tenderly be led by the nose . . .
As asses are.
I have 't, it is engender'd.   Hell and night
Must bring this monstrous birth to the world's light.

Exit

Act Second

SCENE I

A seaport in Cyprus.   An open place near the quay

Enter Montano and two Gentlemen

Mon. What from the cape can you discern at sea ?

1.G. Nothing at all, it is a high-wrought flood,
    I cannot 'twixt the heaven and the main
    Descry a sail.

Mon. Methinks the wind does speak aloud at land ;
    A fuller blast ne'er shook our battlements :
    If it hath ruffian'd so upon the sea,
    What ribs of oak, when the huge mountain melts,
    Can hold the mortise ?   What shall we hear of this ?

2.G. A segregation of the Turkish fleet :   10
    For do but stand upon the foaming shore,   †
    The chiding billow seems to pelt the clouds ;
    The wind-shak'd surge, with high and monstrous mane,
    Seems to cast water on the burning bear,
    And quench the guards of the ever-fixed pole :
    I never did like molestation view
    On the enchafed flood.

Mon. If that the Turkish fleet
  Be not enshelter'd and embay'd, they are drown'd ;
  It is impossible they bear it out.

     Enter a third Gentleman

3.G. News, lads ! your wars are done :   20
  The desperate tempest hath so bang'd the Turk,
  That their designment halts : a noble ship of Venice
  Hath seen a grievous wreck and sufferance
  On most part of their fleet.

Mon. How, is this true ?

3.G.   The ship is here put in,
  A Veronesa ; Michael Cassio,
  Lieutenant to the warlike Moor Othello,
  Is come ashore : the Moor himself at sea,
  And is in full commission here for Cyprus.

Mon. I am glad on 't, 'tis a worthy governor.   30

3.G. But this same Cassio, though he speak of comfort
  Touching the Turkish loss, yet he looks sadly
  And prays the Moor be safe, for they were parted
  With foul and violent tempest.

Mon.   Pray heaven he be ;
  For I have serv'd him, and the man commands
  Like a full soldier. Let 's to the seaside, ho,
  As well to see the vessel that 's come in
  As to throw out our eyes for brave Othello,

{Even till we make the main and the aerial blue
An indistinct regard.}

3.G.   Come, let 's do so ;   40
For every minute is expectancy
Of more arrivance.

Enter Cassio

Cas. Thanks to the valiant of this worthy isle,
That so approve the Moor, and let the heavens
Give him defence against the elements,
For I have lost him on a dangerous sea.

Mon. Is he well shipp'd ?

Cas. His bark is stoutly timber'd, and his pilot
Of very expert and approv'd allowance ;
Therefore my hopes, not surfeited to death,   50
Stand in bold cure.

A cry within : ' A sail, a sail, a sail ! '
Enter a Messenger

What noise ?

Mes. The town is empty ; on the brow o' the sea
Stand ranks of people, and they cry ' A sail ! '

Cas. My hopes do shape him for the governor.   *A shot* †

2.G. They do discharge the shot of courtesy ;
Our friend at least.

Cas.   I pray you, sir, go forth,
And give us truth, who 'tis that is arrived.

2.*G.* I shall.   *Exit*

Mon. But, good lieutenant, is your general wiv'd ?   60

Cas. Most fortunately ; he hath achiev'd a maid

     That paragons description, and wild fame :

     One that excels the {quirks of} blazoning pens,   †

     And in the essential vesture of creation

     Does bear all excellency. . . .

Re-enter second Gentleman

     {How} now, who has put in ?

2.*G.* 'Tis one Iago, ancient to the general.

{*Cas.*} He has had most favourable and happy speed :

     Tempests themselves, high seas, and howling winds,

     The gutter'd rocks, and congregated sands,   70

     Traitors ensteep'd to clog the guiltless keel,

     As having sense of beauty, do omit

     Their common natures, letting go safely by

     The divine Desdemona.

Mon.   What is she ?

Cas. She that I speak of, our great captain's captain,

     Left in the conduct of the bold Iago ;

     Whose footing here anticipates our thoughts

     A se'nnight's speed. . . . Great Jove, Othello guard,

     And swell his sail with thine own powerful breath,

     That he may bless this bay with his tall ship.   80

     And swiftly come to Desdemona's arms,   †

36

Give renew'd fire to our extincted spirits,
[And bring all Cyprus comfort.]

Enter Desdemona, Emilia, Iago, Roderigo, and Attendants

               O, behold,
The riches of the ship is come ashore !
Ye men of Cyprus, let her have your knees :
Hail to thee, lady ! and the grace of heaven,
Before, behind thee, and on every hand,
Enwheel thee round !

Des.   I thank you, valiant Cassio.
What tidings can you tell me of my lord ?

Cas. He is not yet arriv'd : nor know I aught,   90
But that he's well, and will be shortly here.

Des. O, but I fear—How lost you company ?

        A cry within : ' A sail, a sail ! '   *Guns heard*

Cas. The great contention of the sea and skies
Parted our fellowship—But hark, a sail.

2.G. They give their greeting to the citadel :
This likewise is a friend.

Cas.   So speaks this voice.

                  Exit Gentleman

Good ancient, you are welcome. *(to Em.)* Welcome,
   mistress :
Let it not gall your patience, good Iago,
That I extend my manners ; 'tis my breeding

That gives me this bold show of courtesy.   100

Kissing her

Iago. Sir, would she give you so much of her lips
As of her tongue she has bestow'd on me,
You 'ld have enough.

Des.   Alas, she has no speech.

Iago. I know too much ;
I find it, I ; for when I ha' list to sleep—
Marry, before your ladyship, I grant,
She puts her tongue a little in her heart,
And chides with thinking.

Em. You ha' little cause to say so.

Iago. Come on, come on ; you are pictures out of doors,   110
Bells in your parlours ; wild-cats in your kitchens ;
Saints in your injuries ; devils being offended ;
Players in your housewifery ; and housewives in your
        beds.

Des. O, fie upon thee, slanderer !

Iago. Nay, it is true, or else I am a Turk :
You rise to play, and go to bed to work.

Em. You shall not write my praise.

Iago.   No, let me not.

Des. What wouldst thou write of me, if thou shouldst
        praise me ?

Iago. O gentle lady, do not put me to 't,

For I am nothing if not critical.   120

Des. Come on, assay. . . . There 's one gone to the
  harbour ?

Iago. Ay, madam.

Des. I am not merry, but I do beguile
  The thing I am by seeming otherwise :
  Come, how wouldst thou praise me ?

Iago. I am about it, but indeed my invention
  Comes from my pate as birdlime does from freeze ;
  It plucks out brain and all : but my Muse labours,
  And thus she is deliver'd.
  If she be fair and wise, fairness and wit,   130
  The one 's for use, the other useth it.

Des. Well prais'd !   How if she be black and witty ?

Iago. If she be black, and thereto have a wit,
  She 'll find a white that shall her blackness hit.

Des. Worse and worse.

Em. How if fair and foolish ?

Iago. She never yet was foolish that was fair,
  For even her folly help'd her, to an heir.

Des. These are old {fond} paradoxes to make fools laugh
  i' the alehouse.   What miserable praise hast thou   140
  for her that 's foul and foolish ?

Iago. There 's none so foul, and foolish thereunto,
  But does foul pranks which fair and wise ones do.

Des. O heavy ignorance, that praises the worst best : but what praise couldst thou bestow on a deserving woman indeed ? one that in the authority of her merits did justly put on the vouch of very malice itself ?

Iago. She that was ever fair, and never proud,
    Had tongue at will, and yet was never loud,   150
    Never lack'd gold, and yet went never gay,
    Fled from her wish, and yet said ' Now I may ; '
    She that, being anger'd, her revenge being nigh,
    Bade her wrong stay, and her displeasure fly ;
    She that in wisdom never was so frail
    To change the cod's head for the salmon's tail ;
    She that could think, and ne'er disclose her mind,
    {See suitors following and not look behind ;}
    She was a wight, if ever such wight were,—

Des. To do what ?   160

Iago. To suckle fools, and chronicle small beer.

Des. O most lame and impotent conclusion ! Do not learn of him, Emilia, though he be thy husband. How say you, Cassio ? is he not a most profane and liberal counsellor ?

Cas. He speaks home, madam : you may relish him more in the soldier than in the scholar.

Iago. (*aside*) He takes her by the palm : ay, well said,

whisper : {with} as little a web as this will {I}
ensnare as great a fly as Cassio.   Ay, smile upon 170
her, do ; I will catch you in your own courtesies.
You say true, 'tis so, indeed : if such tricks as these
strip you out of your lieutenantry, it had been better
you had not kiss'd your three fingers so oft, which
now again you are most apt to play the sir in.
{Very} good ; well kiss'd ! an excellent courtesy !
'tis so, indeed.   Yet again, your fingers at your lips ?
would they were clyster-pipes for your sake ! . . .
(*Trumpet within.*) The Moor !   I know his trumpet.

Cas. 'Tis truly so.   180

Des. Let's meet him, and receive him.

Cas. Lo, where he comes !

Enter Othello and Attendants

Oth. O my fair warrior !

Des.   My dear Othello !

Oth. It gives me wonder great as my content
　　To see you here before me.   O my soul's joy,
　　If after every tempest come such calmness,
　　May the winds blow till they have waken'd death,
　　And let the labouring bark climb hills of seas,
　　Olympus-high, and duck again as low
　　As hell's from heaven !   If it were now to die,   190
　　'Twere now to be most happy, for I fear

My soul hath her content so absolute,
That not another comfort like to this
Succeeds in unknown fate.

Des.   The heavens forbid
But that our loves and comforts should increase
Even as our days do grow!

Oth.   Amen to that, sweet powers!
I cannot speak enough of this content;
It stops me here, it is too much of joy:
And this, and this, the greatest discords be

                                        They kiss

That e'er our hearts shall make!

Iago.   (*aside*) O, you are well tun'd now, 200
But I'll set down the pegs that make this music,
As honest as I am.

Oth.   Come, let us to the castle.
News, friends; our wars are done, the Turks are
    drown'd.
How do our old acquaintance of the isle?
Honey, you shall be well desir'd in Cyprus;
I have found great love amongst them. O my sweet,
I prattle out of fashion, and I dote
In mine own comforts. I prithee, good Iago,
Go to the bay, and disembark my coffers;
Bring thou the master to the citadel,   210

He is a good one, and his worthiness
Does challenge much respect.   Come, Desdemona,
Once more well met at Cyprus.

Exeunt all but Iago and Roderigo

Iago. Do thou meet me presently at the harbour.   Come
hither ; if thou be'st valiant—as, they say, base men
being in love have then a nobility in their natures
more than is native to them . . . list me, the
lieutenant to-night watches on the court of guard.
First, I will tell thee this : Desdemona is directly in
love with him.   220

Rod. With him ? why, 'tis not possible.

Iago. Lay thy finger thus, and let thy soul be instructed.
Mark me with what violence she first loved the
Moor, but for bragging, and telling her fantastical
lies : and will she love him still for prating ? let not
the discreet heart think so.   Her eye must be fed ;
and what delight shall she have to look on the devil ?
When the blood is made dull with the act of sport,
there should be again to inflame it and give satiety
a fresh appetite, loveliness in favour, sympathy in   230
years, manners and beauties ; all which the Moor is
defective in : now, for want of these requir'd con-
veniences, her delicate tenderness will find itself
abus'd, begin to heave the gorge, disrelish and abhor

43

the Moor; very nature will instruct her to it, and compel her to some second choice. Now, sir, this granted—as it is a most pregnant and unforc'd position—who stands so eminently in the degree of this fortune as Cassio does? a knave very voluble, no further conscionable than in putting on the mere 240 form of civil and humane seeming for the better compassing of his salt and {most} hidden {loose} affections? {why, none; why, none:} a subtle slippery knave; a finder out of occasions; that has an eye, can stamp and counterfeit the true advantages never present themselves: {a devilish knave!} Besides, the knave is handsome, young, and hath all those requisites in him that folly and green minds look after; a pestilent complete knave, and the woman has found him already. 250

Rod. I cannot believe that in her, she's full of most blest condition.

Iago. Blest fig's end! the wine she drinks is made of grapes: if she had been blest she would never have lov'd the Moor: {blest pudding!} Didst thou not see her paddle with the palm of his hand? {didst not mark that?}

Rod. Yes, {that I did:} but that was but courtesy.

Iago. Lechery, by this hand; an index and {obscure} pro-

logue to the history of lust and foul thoughts. They 260
met so near with their lips that their breaths em-
braced together.   {Villanous thoughts, Roderigo!}
when these mutualities so marshal the way, hard at
hand comes the {master and} main exercise, the
incorporate conclusion: {pish!} But, sir, be you
rul'd by me, I have brought you from Venice.
Watch you to-night; for your command, I'll lay't
upon you; Cassio knows you not, I'll not be far
from you, do you find some occasion to anger
Cassio, either by speaking too loud, or tainting his 270
discipline, or from what other cause you please,
which the time shall more favourably minister.

Rod. Well.

Iago. Sir, he is rash, and very sudden in choler, and haply
[with his truncheon] may strike at you: provoke
him that he may, for even out of that will I cause
these of Cyprus to mutiny, whose qualification shall
come into no true trust again but by the displanting
of Cassio. So shall you have a shorter journey to
your desires by the means I shall then have to prefer 280
them, and the impediment most profitably remov'd,
without which there were no expectation of our
prosperity.

Rod. I will do this, if I can bring it to any opportunity.

Iago. I warrant thee.   Meet me by and by at the citadel :
    I must fetch his necessaries ashore. . . . Farewell.

Rod. Adieu.   *Exit*

Iago. That Cassio loves her, I do well believe it ;
    That she loves him, 'tis apt and of great credit :
    The Moor, howbeit that I endure him not,   290
    Is of a constant, loving, noble nature ;
    And I dare think he 'll prove to Desdemona
    A most dear husband.   Now, I do love her too,
    Not out of absolute lust, though peradventure
    I stand accountant for as great a sin,
    But partly led to diet my revenge,
    For that I do suspect the lustful Moor
    Hath leap'd into my seat, the thought whereof
    Doth like a poisonous mineral gnaw my inwards,
    And nothing can nor shall content my soul   300
    Till I am even with him, wife for wife ;
    Or failing so, yet that I put the Moor,
    At least, into a jealousy so strong
    That judgement cannot cure.   Which thing to do,
    If this poor trash of Venice, whom I trash   †
    For his quick hunting, stand the putting on,
    I 'll have our Michael Cassio on the hip,
    Abuse him to the Moor in the rank garb
    (For I fear Cassio with my night-cap too)

Make the Moor thank me, love me, and reward me, 310
For making him egregiously an ass,
And practising upon his peace and quiet,
Even to madness : 'tis here, but yet confus'd :
Knavery's plain face is never seen till us'd.   *Exit*

SCENE II

A street

Enter a Herald with a proclamation ; People following

Her. It is Othello's pleasure ; our noble and valiant †
general, that upon certain tidings now arrived,
importing the mere perdition of the Turkish fleet ;
every man put himself into triumph ; some to dance,
some to make bonfires ; each man to what sport
and revels his mind leads him ; for, besides these
beneficial news, it is the celebration of his nuptials.
So much was his pleasure should be proclaimed.
All offices are open, and there is full liberty, {of
feasting} from this present hour of five, till the   10
bell hath told eleven. Heaven bless the isle of
Cyprus, and our noble general Othello !   *Exeunt*

SCENE III

A hall in the castle

Enter Othello, Desdemona, Cassio, and Attendants

Oth. Good Michael, look you to the guard to-night,
Let's teach ourselves the honourable stop,
Not to outsport discretion.

Cas. Iago hath directed what to do ;
But notwithstanding with my personal eye
Will I look to it.

Oth.   Iago is most honest.
Michael, good night ; to-morrow with your earliest
Let me have speech with you ; come, my dear love,
The purchase made, the fruits are to ensue,
The profit's yet to come 'twixt me and you.   10
Good night.

> *Exeunt Othello, Desdemona, and Attendants*
> *Enter Iago*

Cas. Welcome, Iago, we must to the watch.

Iago. Not this hour, lieutenant ; 'tis not yet ten o' clock : †
our general cast us thus early for the love of his
Desdemona ; who let us not therefore blame ; he
hath not yet made wanton the night with her ; and
she is sport for Jove.

Cas. She is a most exquisite lady.

Iago. And I'll warrant her full of game.

Cas. Indeed she is a most fresh and delicate creature.   20

Iago. What an eye she has ! methinks it sounds a parley
of provocation.

Cas. An inviting eye, and yet methinks right modest.

Iago. And when she speaks, 'tis an alarum to love ?

Cas. It is indeed perfection.

Iago. Well, happiness, to their sheets. . . . Come, lieutenant, I have a stoup of wine, and here without
are a brace of Cyprus gallants that would fain have
a measure to the health of the black Othello.

Cas. Not to-night, good Iago ; I have very poor and   30
unhappy brains for drinking : I could well wish
courtesy would invent some other custom of entertainment.

Iago. O, they are our friends . . . but one cup : I'll
drink for you.

Cas. I ha' drunk but one cup to-night, and that was
craftily qualified too, and behold what innovation
it makes here : I am unfortunate in the infirmity,
and dare not task my weakness with any more.

Iago. What, man, 'tis a night of revels, the gallants desire it.   40

Cas. Where are they ?

Iago. Here at the door ; I pray you, call them in.

Cas. I'll do 't, but it dislikes me.   *Exit*

Iago. If I can fasten but one cup upon him,
    With that which he hath drunk to-night already,
    He 'll be as full of quarrel and offence
    As my young mistress' dog : . . . Now my sick fool
        Roderigo,
    Whom love hath turn'd almost the wrong side out-
        ward
    To Desdemona hath to-night carous'd
    Potations pottle-deep, and he 's to watch :   50
    Three lads of Cyprus, noble swelling spirits,
    That hold their honour in a wary distance,
    The very elements of this warlike isle,
    Have I to-night fluster'd with flowing cups,
    And they watch too.   Now, 'mongst this flock of
        drunkards,
    Am I to put our Cassio in some action
    That may offend the isle.   But here they come :
    If consequence do but approve my dream,
    My boat sails freely, both with wind and stream.
      Re-enter Cassio ; with him Montano and Gentlemen :
         Servants following with wine

Cas. 'Fore God, they have given me a rouse already.   60

Mon. Good faith, a little one ; not past a pint, as I am a
    soldier.

Iago. Some wine, ho !

> (*sings*) And let me the canakin clink, clink
>> And let me the canakin clink, clink :
>>> A soldier 's a man ;
>>> A life 's but a span ;
>> Why then let a soldier drink.

Some wine, boys !

Cas. 'Fore God, an excellent song.

Iago. I learn'd it in England, where indeed they are most   70
potent in potting : your Dane, your German, and
your swag-bellied Hollander,—Drink, ho !—are
nothing to your English.

Cas. Is your Englishman so expert in his drinking ?

Iago. Why, he drinks you with facility your Dane dead
drunk ; he sweats not to overthrow your Almain ;
he gives your Hollander a vomit ere the next pottle
can be filled.

Cas. To the health of our general !

Mon. I am for it, lieutenant, and I will do you justice.   80

Iago. O sweet England !

> (*sings*) King Stephen was a worthy peer,
>> His breeches cost him but a crown ;
> He held them sixpence all too dear,
>> With that he call'd the tailor lown.

51

He was a wight of high renown,
  And thou art but of low degree :
'Tis pride that pulls the country down ;
  Then take thine owd cloak about thee.
 Some wine, ho !   90

Cas. 'Fore God, this is a more exquisite song than the
 other.

Iago. Will you hear 't again ?

Cas. No, for I hold him unworthy of his place that does
 those things : well, God 's above all, and there be
 souls that must be saved, {and there be souls must
 not be saved.}

Iago. It is true, good lieutenant.

Cas. For mine own part, no offence to the general, nor any
 man of quality, I hope to be sav'd.   100

Iago. And so do I lieutenant.

Cas. Ay, but, by your leave, not before me ; the lieutenant
 is to be sav'd before the ancient. Let 's have no
 more of this, let 's to our affairs. God forgive us
 our sins ! Gentlemen, let 's look to our business.
 Do not think, gentlemen, I am drunk, this is my
 ancient, this is my right hand, and this is my left
 hand. I am not drunk now, I can stand well
 enough, and speak well enough.

All. Excellent well.   110

Cas. Very well then; you must not think that I am drunk.

Exit

Mon. To the platform, masters.   Come, let's set the watch.

Iago. You see this fellow that is gone before;

He is a soldier fit to stand by Cæsar,

And give direction : and do but see his vice,

'Tis to his virtue a just equinox,

The one as long as the other : 'tis pity of him.

I fear the trust Othello put him in,

On some odd time of his infirmity,

Will shake this island.

Mon.   But is he often thus ?   120

Iago. 'Tis evermore the prologue to his sleep :

He 'll watch the horologe a double set,

If drink rock not his cradle.

Mon.   It were well

The general were put in mind of it.

Perhaps he sees it not, or his good nature

Prizes the virtues that appears in Cassio

And looks not on his evils : is not this true ?

Enter Roderigo

Iago. (*aside to him*) How now, Roderigo ?

I pray you, after the lieutenant, go. [*Exit Roderigo*]

Mon. And 'tis great pity that the noble Moor   130

Should hazard such a place as his own second

With one of an ingraft infirmity :
It were an honest action to say
So to the Moor.

Iago.   Not I, for this fair island :

                    A cry within : ' Help ! help ! '
I do love Cassio well, and would do much
To cure him of this evil :—But, hark ! what noise ?

      Re-enter Cassio, driving in Roderigo

Cas. 'Zounds ! you rogue ! you rascal !

Mon. What 's the matter, lieutenant ?

Cas. A knave teach me my duty ! But I 'll beat the
    knave into a wicker bottle.   140

Rod. Beat me ?

Cas. Dost thou prate, rogue ?   *Striking Roderigo*

Mon. Good lieutenant ; pray, sir, hold your hand.

Cas. Let me go, sir, or I 'll knock you o'er the mazzard.

Mon. Come, come, you 're drunk.

Cas. Drunk ?   [*They fight*]

Iago. (*aside to Rod.*) Away, I say ; go out and cry a
      mutiny.   *Exit Roderigo*

    Nay, good lieutenant ! God's will, gentlemen !
    Help, ho !—Lieutenant,—sir,—Montano,—sir ;—
    Help, masters !—Here 's a goodly watch indeed !   150

                        [*A bell rings*]

    Who 's that that rings the bell ?—Diablo, ho !

The town will rise : God's will, lieutenant, hold ;
You will be sham'd for ever.

Re-enter Othello and Attendants

Oth.   What is the matter here ?

Mon.'Zounds, I bleed still ; I am hurt to the death.

Faints

Oth. Hold, for your lives !

Iago. Hold, hold ! Lieutenant,—sir,—Montano,—gentle-
          men,—

Have you forgot all sense of place and duty ?

Hold ! the general speaks to you ; hold, hold, for
          shame !

Oth. Why, how now, ho ! from whence ariseth this ?
Are we turn'd Turks, and to ourselves do that   160
Which heaven has forbid the Ottomites ?
For Christian shame, put by this barbarous brawl :
He that stirs next, to carve for his own rage,
Holds his soul light, he dies upon his motion.
Silence that dreadful bell, it frights the isle
From her propriety.   What 's the matter, masters ?
Honest Iago, that looks dead with grieving,
Speak, who began this ? on thy love, I charge thee.

Iago. I do not know ; friends all but now, even now,
In quarter, and in terms like bride and groom   170
Devesting them to bed ; and then, but now,

As if some planet had unwitted men,
Swords out, and tilting one at other's breast,
In opposition bloody.   I cannot speak
Any beginning to this peevish odds ;
And would in action glorious I had lost
These legs that brought me to a part of it !

Oth. How came it, Michael, you were thus forgot ?

Cas. I pray you, pardon me, I cannot speak.

Oth. Worthy Montano, you were wont be civil ;   180
The gravity and stillness of your youth
The world hath noted, and your name is great
In mouths of wisest censure : what 's the matter,
That you unlace your reputation thus,
And spend your rich opinion for the name
Of a night-brawler ? give me answer to 't.

Mon. Worthy Othello, I am hurt to danger :
Your officer, Iago, can inform you—
While I spare speech, which something now offends
   me—
Of all that I do know, nor know I aught   190
By me that 's said or done amiss this night,
Unless self-charity be sometimes a vice,
And to defend ourselves it be a sin
When violence assails us.

Oth   Now, by heaven,

56

My blood begins my safer guides to rule,
And passion, having my best judgement collied,   †
Assays to lead the way : zounds, if I stir,
Or do but lift this arm, the best of you
Shall sink in my rebuke.   Give me to know
How this foul rout began, who set it on,   200
And he that is approv'd in this offence,
Though he had twinn'd with me, both at a birth,
Shall lose me.   What ? in a town of war,
Yet wild, the people's hearts brimful of fear,
To manage private and domestic quarrels,
In night, and on the court and guard of safety !
'Tis monstrous.   Iago, who began ?

Mon. If partially affin'd, or leagu'd in office,
Thou dost deliver more or less than truth,
Thou art no soldier.

Iago.   Touch me not so near :   210
I had rather have this tongue cut from my mouth
Than it should do offence to Michael Cassio ;
Yet, I persuade myself, to speak the truth
Shall nothing wrong him.   Thus it is, general.
Montano and myself being in speech,
There comes a fellow, crying out for help,
And Cassio following him with determin'd sword,
To execute upon him.   Sir, this gentleman

Steps in to Cassio, and entreats his pause ;
Myself the crying fellow did pursue,   220
Lest by his clamour, as it so fell out,
The town might fall in fright : he, swift of foot.
Outran my purpose ; and I return'd the rather
For that I heard the clink and fall of swords,
And Cassio high in oath, which till to-night
I ne'er might see before.   When I came back—
For this was brief—I found them close together,
At blow and thrust, even as again they were
When you yourself did part them.
More of this matter can I not report :   230
But men are men, the best sometimes forget ;
Though Cassio did some little wrong to him,
As men in rage strike those that wish them best,
Yet surely Cassio, I believe, receiv'd
From him that fled some strange indignity,
Which patience could not pass.

Oth.   I know, Iago,
Thy honesty and love doth mince this matter,
Making it light to Cassio.   Cassio, I love thee,
But never more be officer of mine.

Re-enter Desdemona, attended

Look, if my gentle love be not rais'd up !   240
I 'll make thee an example.

Des.   What's the matter?

Oth. All's well now, sweeting ; come away to bed.

Sir, for your hurts, myself will be your surgeon :

To Montano, who is led off

Lead him off.

Iago, look with care about the town,

And silence those whom this vile brawl distracted.

Come, Desdemona : 'tis the soldiers' life

To have their balmy slumbers wak'd with strife.

Exeunt all but Iago and Cassio

Iago. What, are you hurt, lieutenant?

Cas. Ay, past all surgery.   250

Iago. Marry, God forbid!

Cas. Reputation, reputation, {reputation! O,} I have
lost my reputation! I have lost the immortal part,
sir, of myself, and what remains is bestial. My
reputation, Iago, my reputation!

Iago. As I am an honest man, I thought you had receiv'd
some bodily wound ; there is more offence in that
than in reputation. Reputation is an idle and most
false imposition, oft got without merit and lost
without deserving. You have lost no reputation   260
at all, unless you repute yourself such a loser ; what,
man, there are ways to recover the general again :
you are but now cast in his mood, a punishment

59

more in policy than in malice, even so as one would
beat his offenceless dog to affright an imperious
lion : sue to him again, and he 's yours.

Cas. I will rather sue to be despis'd than to deceive so
good a commander with so light, so drunken, and
so indiscreet an officer. {Drunk? and speak par-
rot? and squabble? swagger? swear? and dis- 270
course fustian with one's own shadow?} O thou
invisible spirit of wine, if thou hast no name to be
known by, let us call thee devil !

Iago. What was he that you follow'd with your sword?
What had he done to you?

Cas. I know not.

Iago. Is't possible?

Cas. I remember a mass of things, but nothing distinctly ;
a quarrel, but nothing wherefore. O God, that
men should put an enemy in their mouths, to steal 280
away their brains ; that we should, with joy, revel,
pleasure, and applause, transform ourselves into
beasts !

Iago. Why, but you are now well enough : how came
you thus recover'd?

Cas. It hath pleas'd the devil drunkenness to give place
to the devil wrath : one unperfectness shows me
another, to make me frankly despise myself.

Iago. Come, you are too severe a moraler : as the time, the
place, the condition of this country stands, I could 290
heartily wish this had not so befallen ; but since it is
as it is, mend it, for your own good.

Cas. I will ask him for my place again : he shall tell me
I am a drunkard !   Had I as many mouths as Hydra,
such an answer would stop them all : to be now a
sensible man, by and by a fool, and presently a
beast !   {O strange !}   Every unordinate cup is un-
blest, and the ingredience is a devil.

Iago. Come, come, good wine is a good familiar creature,
if it be well us'd : exclaim no more against it.   And, 300
good lieutenant, I think you think I love you.

Cas. I have well approv'd it, sir, . . . I drunk !

Iago. You, or any man living may be drunk at some time.
I 'll tell you what you shall do. . . . Our general's
wife is now the general : I may say so in this respect,
for that he has devoted and given up himself to
the contemplation, mark and denotement of her
parts and graces.   Confess yourself freely to her,
importune she 'll help to put you in your place
again : she is so free, so kind, so apt, so blessed a 310
disposition, she holds it a vice in her goodness not
to do more than she is requested : this broken joint †
between you and her husband entreat her to splinter ;

and, my fortunes against any lay worth naming, this
crack of your love shall grow stronger than 't was
before.

Cas. You advise me well.

Iago. I protest, in the sincerity of love and honest kindness.

Cas. I think it freely, and betimes in the morning will I
    beseech the virtuous Desdemona to undertake for 320
    me : I am desperate of my fortunes, if they check
    me here.

Iago. You are in the right.
    Good night, lieutenant ; I must to the watch.

Cas. Good night, honest Iago.   *Exit*

Iago. And what's he then that says I play the villain,
    When this advice is free I give and honest,
    Probal to thinking, and indeed the course
    To win the Moor again ? For 'tis most easy
    The inclining Desdemona to subdue   330
    In any honest suit ; she's fram'd as fruitful
    As the free elements, and then for her
    To win the Moor, were 't to renounce his baptism,
    All seals and symbols of redeemed sin,
    His soul is so infetter'd to her love,
    That she may make, unmake, do what she list,
    Even as her appetite shall play the god
    With his weak function : how am I then a villain

To counsel Cassio to this parallel course,
Directly to his good ?   Divinity of hell !   340
When devils will their blackest sins put on,
They do suggest at first with heavenly shows,
As I do now : for while this honest fool
Plies Desdemona to repair his fortunes,
And she for him pleads strongly to the Moor,
I'll pour this pestilence into his ear,
That she repeals him for her body's lust ;
And by how much she strives to do him good,
She shall undo her credit with the Moor.
So will I turn her virtue into pitch,   350
And out of her own goodness make the net
That shall enmesh them all.

Enter Roderigo

               How now, Roderigo ?

Rod. I do follow here in the chase, not like a hound that
hunts, but one that fills up the cry.   My money is
almost spent, I have been to-night exceedingly well
cudgel'd ; I think the issue will be, I shall have so
much experience for my pains as that comes to,
and no money at all, and with that wit return to
Venice.

Iago. How poor are they that have not patience !   360
What wound did ever heal, but by degrees ?

Thou know'st we work by wit, and not by witchcraft,
And wit depends on dilatory time.
Does't not go well ? Cassio hath beaten thee,
And thou, by that small hurt, hast cashier'd Cassio :
Though other things grow fair against the sun,
Yet fruits that blossom first will first be ripe :
Content thyself awhile. By the mass, 'tis morning ;
Pleasure and action make the hours seem short.
Retire thee ; go where thou art billeted :   370
Away, I say, thou shalt know more hereafter :
Nay, get thee gone. (*exit Rod.*) Two things are to
    be done :
My wife must move for Cassio to her mistress ;
I 'll set her on ;
Myself the while to draw the Moor apart,
And bring him jump when he may Cassio find
Soliciting his wife : ay, that 's the way :
Dull not device by coldness and delay.   *Exit*

Act Third

SCENE I

Before the castle

Enter Cassio and some Musicians

Cas. Masters, play here, I will content your pains ;
    Something that 's brief, and bid ' Good morrow,
      general.'   *Music*

Enter Clown

Clo. Why, masters, have your instruments been at
    Naples, that they speak i' the nose thus ?

1.M. How, sir, how ?

Clo. Are these, I pray you, call'd wind-instruments ?

1.M. Ay, marry, are they, sir.

Clo. O, thereby hangs a tail.

1.M. Whereby hangs a tale, sir ?

Clo. Marry, sir, by many a wind-instrument that I know.   10
    But, masters, here 's money for you : and the general
    so likes your music, that he desires you, of all loves,
    to make no more noise with it.

1.M. Well, sir, we will not.

Clo. If you have any music that may not be heard, to 't

again : but, as they say, to hear music the general
does not greatly care.

1.M. We have none such, sir.

Clo. Then put up your pipes in your bag, for I 'll away :
go ; vanish {into air} ; away !   *Exeunt Musicians*   20

Cas. Dost thou hear my honest friend ?   †

Clo. No, I hear not your honest friend, I hear you.

Cas. Prithee, keep up thy quillets ; there 's a poor piece
of gold for thee : if the gentlewoman that attends
the general's wife be stirring, tell her there 's one
Cassio entreats her a little favour of speech . . . wilt
thou do this ?

Clo. She is stirring, sir, if she will stir hither, I shall
seem to notify unto her.

Cas. [Do, good my friend.]   *Exit Clown*

Enter Iago

In happy time, Iago.   30

Iago. You have not been a-bed, then ?

Cas. Why, no ; the day had broke
Before we parted.   I have made bold, Iago,
To send in to your wife, . . . my suit to her
Is, that she will to virtuous Desdemona
Procure me some access.

Iago.   I 'll send her to you presently,
And I 'll devise a mean to draw the Moor

Out of the way, that your converse and business
May be more free.

Cas. I humbly thank you for 't. (*exit Iago.*) I never knew 40
A Florentine more kind and honest.

Enter Emilia

Em. Good morrow, good lieutenant, I am sorry
For your displeasure, but all will sure be well ;
The general and his wife are talking of it,
And she speaks for you stoutly : the Moor replies,
That he you hurt is of great fame in Cyprus
And great affinity, and that in wholesome wisdom
He might not but refuse you ; but he protests he
        loves you,
And needs no other suitor but his likings
To take the safest occasion by the front   50
To bring you in again.

Cas.   Yet, I beseech you,
If you think fit, or that it may be done,
Give me advantage of some brief discourse
With Desdemona alone.

Em.   Pray you, come in :
I will bestow you where you shall have time
To speak your bosom freely.

{*Cas.*   I am much bound to you}
                                             Exeunt

SCENE II

A room in the castle

Enter Othello, Iago, and Gentlemen

Oth. These letters give, Iago, to the pilot,
And by him do my duties to the State:
That done, I will be walking on the works;
Repair there to me.

Iago.　　　　　Well, my good lord, I'll do 't.

Oth. This fortification, gentlemen, shall we see 't?

Gen. We wait upon your lordship.　　　　　*Exeunt*

SCENE III

The garden of the castle

Enter Desdemona, Cassio, and Emilia

Des. Be thou assur'd, good Cassio, I will do
All my abilities in thy behalf.

Em. Good madam, do: I know it grieves my husband
As if the case were his.

Des. O, that's an honest fellow:—do not doubt, Cassio,
But I will have my lord and you again
As friendly as you were.

Cas.   Bounteous madam,
 Whatever shall become of Michael Cassio,
 He's never any thing but your true servant.

Des. O sir, I thank you.   You do love my lord,   10
 You have known him long, and be you well assur'd
 He shall in strangest stand no farther off
 Than in a politic distance.

Cas.   Ay, but, lady,
 The policy may either last so long,
 Or feed upon such nice and waterish diet,
 Or breed itself so out of circumstance,
 That, I being absent, and my place supplied,
 My general will forget my love and service.

Des. Do not doubt that ; before Emilia here
 I give thee warrant of thy place ; assure thee.   20
 If I do vow a friendship, I 'll perform it
 To the last article ; my lord shall never rest,
 I 'll watch him tame, and talk him out of patience ;
 His bed shall seem a school, his board a shrift,
 I 'll intermingle every thing he does
 With Cassio's suit ; therefore be merry, Cassio ;
 For thy solicitor shall rather die
 Than give thy cause away.

          Enter Othello and Iago, at a distance

Em. Madam, here comes my lord.

Cas. Madam, I 'll take my leave.   30

Des. Why, stay and hear me speak.

Cas. Madam, not now, I am very ill at ease,
    Unfit for mine own purpose.

Des. Well, do your discretion.   *Exit Cassio*

Iago. Ha, I like not that.

Oth. What dost thou say ?

Iago. Nothing, my lord, or if—I know not what.

Oth. Was not that Cassio parted from my wife ?

Iago. Cassio, my lord ? . . . No, sure, I cannot think it,
    That he would sneak away so guilty-like,   40
    Seeing you coming.

Oth.   I do believe 'twas he.

Des. How now, my lord ?
    I have been talking with a suitor here.
    A man that languishes in your displeasure.

Oth. Who is 't you mean ?

Des. Why, your lieutenant, Cassio ; good my lord,
    If I have any grace or power to move you,
    His present reconciliation take ;
    For if he be not one that truly loves you,
    That errs in ignorance, and not in cunning,   50
    I have no judgement in an honest face ;
    I prithee, call him back.

Oth.   Went he hence now ?

Des. Yes, faith, so humbled,
   That he has left part of his griefs with me ;
   I suffer with him ; good love, call him back.
Oth. Not now, sweet Desdemona, some other time.
Des. But shall 't be shortly ?
Oth.   The sooner, sweet, for you.
Des. Shall 't be to-night at supper ?
Oth.   No, not to-night.
Des. To-morrow dinner then ?
Oth.   I shall not dine at home,
   I meet the captains, at the citadel.   60
Des. Why then to-morrow night, or Tuesday morn,
   On Tuesday morn, or night, or Wednesday morn,   †
   I prithee, name the time, but let it not
   Exceed three days : in faith, he 's penitent,
   And yet his trespass, in our common reason
   (Save that, they say, the wars must make examples
   Out of their best) is not almost a fault
   To incur a private check.   When shall he come ?
   Tell me, Othello : I wonder in my soul,
   What you would ask me, that I should deny,   70
   Or stand so mammering on.   What ! Michael Cassio ?
   That came a-wooing with you, and so many a time,
   When I have spoke of you dispraisingly,
   Hath ta'en your part, to have so much to do

     To bring him in? By 'r lady, I could do much—

Oth. Prithee, no more, let him come when he will,
     I will deny thee nothing.

Des.   Why, this is not a boon;
     'Tis as I should entreat you wear your gloves,
     Or feed on nourishing dishes, or keep you warm,
     Or sue to you to do a peculiar profit   80
     To your own person: nay, when I have a suit
     Wherein I mean to touch your love indeed,
     It shall be full of poise and difficulty,
     And fearful to be granted.

Oth.   I will deny thee nothing,
     Whereon, I do beseech thee, grant me this,
     To leave me but a little to myself.

Des. Shall I deny you? no: farewell, my lord.

Oth. Farewell, my Desdemona, I'll come to thee straight,

Des. Emilia, come; be it as your fancies teach you;
     Whate'er you be, I am obedient.   90

                       Exeunt Desdemona and Emilia

Oth. Excellent wretch! Perdition catch my soul,
     But I do love thee, and when I love thee not,
     Chaos is come again.

Iago. My noble lord,—

Oth.   What dost thou say, Iago?

Iago. Did Michael Cassio, when you woo'd my lady,

Know of your love ?

Oth. He did, from first to last : . . . why dost thou ask ?

Iago. But for a satisfaction of my thoughts . . . ;
No further harm.

Oth.   Why of thy thought, Iago ?

Iago. I did not think he had been acquainted with her.   100

Oth. O, yes, and went between us very often.

Iago. Indeed !

Oth. Indeed ! ay, indeed : discern'st thou aught in that ?
Is he not honest ?

Iago. Honest, my lord ?

Oth. Honest ! ay, honest.

Iago. My lord, for aught I know.

Oth. What dost thou think ?

Iago. Think, my lord ?

Oth. Think, my lord ! By heaven, he echoes me,   110
As if there were some monster in his thought
Too hideous to be shown.   Thou didst mean some-
          thing :
I heard thee say but now, thou lik'st not that,
When Cassio left my wife : what didst not like ?
And when I told thee he was of my counsel
In my whole course of wooing, thou criedst ' Indeed ? '
And didst contract and purse thy brow together,
As if thou then hadst shut up in thy brain

Some horrible conceit : if thou dost love me,
Show me thy thought.   120
Iago. My lord, you know I love you.
Oth.   I think thou dost ;
And for I know thou 'rt full of love and honesty
And weigh'st thy words before thou give 'em breath,
Therefore these stops of thine fright me the more :
For such things in a false disloyal knave
Are tricks of custom ; but in a man that 's just
They 're close denotements, working from the heart,
That passion cannot rule.
Iago.   For Michael Cassio,
I dare be sworn I think that he is honest.
Oth. I think so too.
Iago.   Men should be that they seem ;   130
Or those that be not, would they might seem none !
Oth. Certain, men should be what they seem.
Iago. Why then I think Cassio 's an honest man.
Oth. Nay, yet there 's more in this :
I prithee, speak to me as to thy thinkings,
As thou dost ruminate, and give the worst of thought
The worst of word.
Iago.   Good my lord, pardon me :
Though I am bound to every act of duty,
I am not bound to that all slaves are free to.

Utter my thoughts ?   Why, say they are vile and false ;
As where's that palace, whereinto foul things   141
Sometimes intrude not ? who has a breast so pure,
But some uncleanly apprehensions
Keep leets and law-days, and in session sit
With meditations lawful ?

Oth. Thou dost conspire against thy friend, Iago,
If thou but think'st him wrong'd, and mak'st his ear
A stranger to thy thoughts.

Iago.   I do beseech you—
Though I perchance am vicious in my guess,
As, I confess, it is my nature's plague   150
To spy into abuses, and oft my jealousy
Shapes faults that are not—I entreat you then,   †
From one that so imperfectly conjects,
You 'ld take no notice, nor build yourself a trouble
Out of my scattering and unsure observance ;
It were not for your quiet, nor your good,
Nor for my manhood, honesty, or wisdom,
To let you know my thoughts.

Oth.   Zounds !

Iago. Good name in man and woman's dear, my lord,
Is the immediate jewel of our souls :   160
Who steals my purse steals trash, 'tis something,
          nothing,

'Twas mine, 'tis his, and has been slave to thousands ;
But he that filches from me my good name
Robs me of that which not enriches him
And makes me poor indeed.

Oth. By heaven, I 'll know thy thought.

Iago. You cannot, if my heart were in your hand,
    Nor shall not, whilst 'tis in my custody.

{*Oth.*Ha !

Iago.}   O, beware, {my lord, of} jealousy ;
    It is the green-eyed monster, which doth mock   †
    That meat it feeds on : that cuckold lives in bliss   171
    Who, certain of his fate, loves not his wronger ;
    But, O, what damned minutes tells he o'er
    Who dotes, yet doubts, suspects, yet strongly loves !

Oth. O misery !

Iago. Poor and content is rich, and rich enough,
    But riches fineless is as poor as winter
    To him that ever fears he shall be poor :
    Good God, the souls of all my tribe defend
    From jealousy !

Oth.   Why, why is this ?   180
    Think'st thou I 'ld make a life of jealousy,
    To follow still the changes of the moon
    With fresh suspicions ? No, to be once in doubt
    Is once to be resolv'd : exchange me for a goat,

When I shall turn the business of my soul
To such exsufflicate and blown surmises,
Matching thy inference.   'Tis not to make me jealous
To say my wife is fair, feeds well, loves company,
Is free of speech, sings, plays and dances well ;
Where virtue is, these are more virtuous :   190
Nor from mine own weak merits will I draw
The smallest fear, or doubt of her revolt,
For she had eyes, and chose me.   No, Iago ;
I 'll see before I doubt, when I doubt, prove,
And on the proof, there is no more but this :
Away at once with love or jealousy !

Iago. I am glad of it, for now I shall have reason
To show the love and duty that I bear you
With franker spirit : therefore, as I am bound,
Receive it from me.   I speak not yet of proof.   200
Look to your wife, observe her well with Cassio ;
Wear your eye thus, not jealous, nor secure :
I would not have your free and noble nature
Out of self-bounty be abus'd ; look to 't :
I know our country disposition well,
In Venice they do let God see the pranks
They dare not show their husbands ; their best con-
          science
Is not to leave undone, but keep unknown.

Oth. Dost thou say so ?

Iago. She did deceive her father, marrying you ;   210
　　　And when she seem'd to shake and fear your looks,
　　　She lov'd them most.

Oth.　　　　　　　　And so she did.

Iago.　　　　　　　　　　Why, go to then,
　　　She that so young could give out such a seeming,
　　　To seel her father's eyes up, close as oak—
　　　He thought 'twas witchcraft—but I am much to blame,
　　　I humbly do beseech you of your pardon
　　　For too much loving you.

Oth.　　　　　　　I am bound to thee for ever.

Iago. I see this hath a little dash'd your spirits.

Oth. Not a jot, not a jot.

Iago.　　　　　　I' faith, I fear it has.
　　　I hope you will consider what is spoke   220
　　　Comes from my love ; but I do see you 're moved.
　　　I am to pray you, not to strain my speech
　　　To grosser issues, nor to larger reach
　　　Than to suspicion.

Oth. I will not.

Iago.　　　Should you do so, my lord,
　　　My speech should fall into such vile success
　　　As my thoughts aim not at. Cassio 's my trusty
　　　　friend—

My lord, I see you are mov'd.

Oth.   No, not much mov'd,

I do not think but Desdemona's honest.

Iago. Long live she so, and long live you to think so !   230

Oth. And yet, how nature erring from itself—

Iago. Ay, there 's the point : as, to be bold with you,

Not to affect many proposed matches

Of her own clime, complexion and degree,

Whereto we see in all things nature tends ;

Fie ! one may smell in such a will most rank,

Foul disproportion, thoughts unnatural.

But pardon me : I do not in position

Distinctly speak of her, though I may fear

Her will, recoiling to her better judgement,   240

May fall to match you with her country forms

And happily repent.

Oth.   Farewell ; if more

Thou dost perceive, let me know more, set on

Thy wife to observe : leave me, Iago,

Iago. (*going*) My lord, I take my leave.

Oth. Why did I marry ?   This honest creature doubtless

Sees and knows more, much more, than he unfolds.

Iago. (*returning*) My lord, I would I might entreat your
          honour

To scan this thing no further, leave it to time ;

Though it be fit that Cassio have his place.   250
For sure he fills it up with great ability,
Yet, if you please to hold him off awhile,
You shall by that perceive him and his means :
Note if your lady strain her entertainment
With any strong or vehement importunity ;
Much will be seen in that ; in the mean time,
Let me be thought too busy in my fears,
As worthy cause I have to fear I am ;
And hold her free, I do beseech your honour.

Oth. Fear not my government.   260

Iago. I once more take my leave.   *Exit*

Oth. This fellow's of exceeding honesty,
And knows all qualities, with a learned spirit,
Of human dealing. If I do prove her haggard,
Though that her jesses were my dear heart-strings,
I 'ld whistle her off, and let her down the wind
To prey at fortune. Haply, for I am black
And have not those soft parts of conversation
That chamberers have, or for I am declin'd
Into the vale of years,—yet that 's not much—   270
She 's gone, I am abus'd, and my relief
Must be to loathe her. O curse of marriage,
That we can call these delicate creatures ours,
And not their appetites ! I had rather be a toad,

And live upon the vapour in a dungeon,
Than keep a corner in a thing I love
For others' uses.   Yet, 'tis the plague of great ones ;
Prerogativ'd are they less than the base ;
'Tis destiny, unshunnable, like death :
Even then this forked plague is fated to us   280
When we do quicken.   Desdemona comes :

       Re-enter Desdemona and Emilia

If she be false, O, then heaven mocks itself !
I 'll not believe it.

Des.   How now, my dear Othello ?
Your dinner, and the generous islanders
By you invited, do attend your presence.

Oth. I am to blame.

Des. Why is your speech so faint ? are you not well ?

Oth. I have a pain upon my forehead, here.

Des. Faith, that 's with watching ; 'twill away again ;
Let me but bind your head, within this hour   290
It will be well again.

Oth.   Your napkin is too little ;

    He puts the handkerchief from him ; and she drops it

Let it alone.   Come, I 'll go in with you.

Des. I am very sorry that you are not well.

               Exeunt Othello and Desdemona

Em. I am glad I have found this napkin :

This was her first remembrance from the Moor :
My wayward husband hath a hundred times
Woo'd me to steal it, but she so loves the token,
For he conjur'd her she should ever keep it,
That she reserves it evermore about her
To kiss and talk to.   I 'll have the work ta'en out,   300
And give 't Iago : what he will do with it
Heaven knows, not I ;
I nothing know, but for his fantasy.

Re-enter Iago

Iago. How now, what do you here alone ?

Em. Do not you chide, I have a thing for you.

Iago. A thing for me ? it is a common thing—

Em. Ha ?

Iago. To have a foolish wife.

Em. O, is that all ?   What will you give me now
For that same handkerchief ?

Iago.   What handkerchief ?   310

Em. What handkerchief !
Why, that the Moor first gave to Desdemona,
That which so often you did bid me steal.

Iago. Hast stolen it from her ?

Em. No, faith ; she let it drop by negligence,
And, to the advantage, I being here took 't up.
Look, here it is.

Iago.   A good wench ; give it me.

Em. What will you do with it, that you have been
    So earnest to have me filch it ?

Iago. (*snatching it*) Why, what 's that to you ?   320

Em If 't be not for some purpose of import,
    Give me 't again : poor lady, she 'll run mad
    When she shall lack it.

Iago. Be not you known on 't ; I have use for it. . . .
    Go, leave me.   *Exit Emilia*
    I will in Cassio's lodging lose this napkin,
    And let him find it : trifles light as air
    Are to the jealous confirmations strong
    As proofs of holy writ : this may do something.
    {The Moor already changes with my poison :}   330
    Dangerous conceits are in their natures poisons,
    Which at the first are scarce found to distaste,
    But with a little act upon the blood
    Burn like the mines of sulphur.   I did say so :
    Look, where he comes !

              Re-enter Othello
                Not poppy, nor mandragora
    Nor all the drowsy syrups of the world,
    Shall ever medicine thee to that sweet sleep
    Which thou ow'dst yesterday.

Oth.   Ha ! ha ! false to me, to me ?

Iago. Why, how now, general? no more of that.

Oth. Avaunt, be gone, thou hast set me on the rack: 340
  I swear 'tis better to be much abus'd
  Than but to know a little.

Iago.   How now, my lord?

Oth. What sense had I of her stol'n hours of lust?
  I saw 't not, thought it not, it harm'd not me:
  I slept the next night well, was free and merry;
  I found not Cassio's kisses on her lips:
  He that is robb'd, not wanting what is stol'n,
  Let him not know 't, and he's not robb'd at all.

Iago. I am sorry to hear this.

Oth. I had been happy, if the general camp,   350
  Pioners, and all, had tasted her sweet body,
  So I had nothing known. O, now for ever
  Farewell the tranquil mind, farewell content;
  Farewell the plumed troop, and the big wars
  That make ambition virtue! O, farewell,
  Farewell the neighing steed, and the shrill trump,
  The spirit-stirring drum, the ear-piercing fife,
  The royal banner, and all quality,
  Pride, pomp, and circumstance of glorious war!
  And, O ye mortal engines, whose wide throats   360
  The immortal Jove's great clamour counterfeit,
  Farewell! Othello's occupation's gone!

Iago. Is 't possible, my lord ?

Oth. Villain, be sure thou prove my love a whore,
Be sure of it, give me the ocular proof,
Or, by the worth of man's eternal soul,
Thou hadst been better have been born a dog
Than answer my wak'd wrath !

Iago.   Is 't come to this ?

Oth. Make me to see 't, or at the least so prove it,
That the probation bear no hinge nor loop   370
To hang a doubt on ; or woe upon thy life !

Iago. My noble lord,—

Oth. If thou dost slander her, and torture me,
Never pray more, abandon all remorse ;
On horror's head horrors accumulate ;
Do deeds to make heaven weep, all earth amaz'd ;
For nothing canst thou to damnation add
Greater than that.

Iago.   O grace !   O heaven defend me !
Are you a man ? have you a soul or sense ?
God buy you, take mine office, . . . O wretched fool, 380
That liv'st to make thine honesty a vice !
O monstrous world, take note, take note, O world,
To be direct and honest is not safe.
I thank you for this profit, and from hence
I 'll love no friend, since love breeds such offence.

Oth. Nay, stay, thou shouldst be honest.

Iago. I should be wise, for honesty 's a fool,
And loses that it works for.

{*Oth.*   By the world,
    I think my wife be honest, and think she is not:
    I think that thou art just, and think thou art not: 390
    I 'll have some proof.   Her name, that was as fresh
    As Dian's visage, is now begrim'd and black
    As mine own face.   If there be cords, or knives,
    Poison, or fire, or suffocating streams,
    I 'll not endure it.   Would I were satisfied!

Iago.} I see, sir, you are eaten up with passion,
    I do repent me that I put it to you.
    You would be satisfied?

Oth.   Would, nay, I will.

Iago. And may, but, how, how satisfied, my lord?
    Would you, the supervisor, grossly gape on?   400
    Behold her topp'd?

Oth.   Death and damnation. . . . O!

Iago. It were a tedious difficulty, I think,
    To bring 'em to that prospect: damn 'em then,
    If ever mortal eyes did see them bolster
    More than their own!   What then? how then?
    What shall I say?   Where 's satisfaction?
    It is impossible you should see this,

86

Were they as prime as goats, as hot as monkeys,
As salt as wolves in pride, and fools as gross
As ignorance made drunk.   But yet, I say,   410
If imputation and strong circumstances,
Which lead directly to the door of truth,
Will give you satisfaction, you may have 't.

Oth. Give me a living reason that she 's disloyal.

Iago. I do not like the office,
But sith I am enter'd into this cause so far,
Prick'd to 't by foolish honesty and love,
I will go on.   I lay with Cassio lately,
And being troubled with a raging tooth,
I could not sleep.   420
There are a kind of men so loose of soul,
That in their sleeps will mutter their affairs ;
One of this kind is Cassio :
In sleep I heard him say ' Sweet Desdemona,
Let us be wary, let us hide our loves ; '   †
And then, sir, would he gripe and wring my hand,
Cry out ' Sweet creature ! ' and then kiss me hard,
As if he pluck'd up kisses by the roots,
That grew upon my lips, then laid his leg
Over my thigh, and sigh'd, and kiss'd, and then   430
Cried ' Cursed fate, that gave thee to the Moor ! '

Oth. O monstrous, monstrous !

Iago.   Nay, this was but his dream.

Oth. But this denoted a foregone conclusion.

Iago. 'Tis a shrewd doubt, though it be but a dream. †
  And this may help to thicken other proofs
  That do demonstrate thinly.

Oth.   I 'll tear her all to pieces.

Iago. Nay, but be wise, yet we see nothing done,
  She may be honest yet.   Tell me but this,
  Have you not sometimes seen a handkerchief
  Spotted with strawberries in your wife's hand ?   440

Oth. I gave her such a one, 'twas my first gift.

Iago. I know not that, but such a handkerchief
  (I am sure it was your wife's) did I to-day
  See Cassio wipe his beard with.

Oth.   If 't be that,—

Iago. If it be that, or any that was hers,
  It speaks against her, with the other proofs.

Oth. O, that the slave had forty thousand lives !
  One is too poor, too weak for my revenge.
  Now do I see 'tis true.   Look here, Iago ;
  All my fond love thus do I blow to heaven, . . . 'tis
      gone.   450
  Arise, black vengeance, from thy hollow cell !
  Yield up, O love, thy crown and hearted throne
  To tyrannous hate !   Swell, bosom, with thy fraught,

For 'tis of aspics' tongues !

Iago.   Pray be content.

Oth. O, blood, Iago, blood !

Iago. Patience, I say, your mind perhaps may change.

Oth. Never, {Iago.   Like to the Pontic sea,
    Whose icy current, and compulsive course,
    Ne'er feels retiring ebb, but keeps due on
    To the Propontic, and the Hellespont ;   460
    Even so my bloody thoughts, with violent pace,
    Shall ne'er look back, ne'er ebb to humble love,
    Till that a capable and wide revenge
    Swallow them up.   Now, by yond marble heaven,}
    In the due reverence of a sacred vow   [*Kneels*]
    I here engage my words.

Iago.   Do not rise yet.   [*Kneels*]
    Witness, you ever-burning lights above,
    You elements that clip us round about,
    Witness that here Iago doth give up
    The execution of his wit, hand, heart,   470
    To wrong'd Othello's service !   Let him command,
    And to obey shall be in me remorse,
    What bloody work soever.   *They rise*

Oth.   I greet thy love :
    Not with vain thanks, but with acceptance bounteous,
    And will upon the instant put thee to 't :

Within these three days let me hear thee say
That Cassio 's not alive.

Iago. My friend is dead ; 'tis done as you request :
But let her live.

Oth.   Damn her, lewd minx : O, damn her !
Come, go with me apart, I will withdraw,   480
To furnish me with some swift means of death
For the fair devil.   Now art thou my lieutenant.

Iago. I am your own for ever.   *Exeunt*

SCENE IV

Before the castle

Enter Desdemona, Emilia, and Clown

Des. Do you know, sirrah, where the Lieutenant Cassio
lies ?

Clo. I dare not say he lies any where.

Des. Why, man ?

Clo. He is a soldier ; and for one to say a soldier lies, is
stabbing.

Des. Go to, where lodges he ?

{*Clo.* To tell you where he lodges, is to tell you where
I lie.

Des. Can any thing be made of this ?}   10

Clo. I know not where he lodges ; and for me to devise
a lodging, and say he lies {here or he lies} there,
were to lie in my throat.

Des. Can you inquire him out, and be edified by report ?

Clo. I will catechize the world for him ; that is, make
questions and by them answer.

Des. Seek him, bid him come hither, tell him I have
mov'd my lord on his behalf and hope all will be
well.

Clo. To do this is within the compass of a man, and 20
therefore I will attempt the doing it. *Exit*

Des. Where should I lose that handkerchief, Emilia ?

Em. I know not, madam.

Des. Believe me, I had rather lose my purse
Full of crusadoes : and, but my noble Moor
Is true of mind, and made of no such baseness
As jealous creatures are, it were enough
To put him to ill thinking.

Em.   Is he not jealous ?

Des. Who, he ? I think the sun where he was born
Drew all such humours from him.

Em.   Look, where he comes. 30

Des. I will not leave him now till Cassio
Be called to him.

Enter Othello

How is 't with you, my lord?

Oth. Well, my good lady. (*aside*) O, hardness to dissemble!
How do you, Desdemona?

Des.   Well, my good lord.

Oth. Give me your hand; this hand is moist, my lady.

Des. It yet has felt no age, nor known no sorrow.

Oth. This argues fruitfulness and liberal heart:
Hot, hot, and moist: this hand of yours requires
A sequester from liberty; fasting and praying,
Much castigation, exercise devout;   40
For here 's a young and sweating devil here,
That commonly rebels. 'Tis a good hand,
A frank one.

Des.   You may, indeed, say so,
For 'twas that hand that gave away my heart.

Oth. A liberal hand: the hearts of old gave hands,
But our new heraldry is hands, not hearts.   †

Des. I cannot speak of this. Come, come, your promise.

Oth. What promise, chuck?

Des. I have sent to bid Cassio come speak with you.

Oth. I have a salt and sullen rheum offends me: 50
Lend me thy handkerchief.

Des. Here, my lord.

Oth. That which I gave you.

Des. I have it not about me.

Oth. Not ?

Des. No, faith, my lord.

Oth. That 's a fault.   That handkerchief
　　Did an Egyptian to my mother give ;
　　She was a charmer, and could almost read
　　The thoughts of people: she told her, while she kept it
　　'Twould make her amiable, and subdue my father　　61
　　Entirely to her love ; but if she lost it
　　Or made a gift of it, my father's eye
　　Should hold her loathly, and his spirits should hunt
　　After new fancies : she dying gave it me,
　　And bid me, when my fate would have me wive,
　　To give it her.   I did so : and take heed on 't ;
　　Make it a darling like your precious eye ;
　　To lose, or give 't away, were such perdition
　　As nothing else could match.

Des.　　　　　　　　　　Is 't possible ?　　70

Oth. 'Tis true, there 's magic in the web of it :
　　A sibyl, that had number'd in the world
　　The sun to course two hundred compasses,
　　In her prophetic fury sew'd the work ;
　　The worms were hallow'd that did breed the silk :
　　And it was dyed in mummy, which the skilful
　　Conserve of maidens' hearts.

Des.   I' faith, is 't true ?

Oth. Most veritable, therefore look to 't well.

Des. Then would to God that I had never seen 't !

Oth. Ha ! wherefore ?   80

Des. Why do you speak so startingly and rash ?

Oth. Is 't lost ? is 't gone ? speak, is it out o' the way ?

Des. Heaven bless us !

Oth. Say you ?

Des. It is not lost, but what an if it were ?

Oth. Ha !

Des. I say, it is not lost.

Oth. Fetch 't, let me see it.

Des. Why, so I can, sir, but I will not now,

     This is a trick to put me from my suit :   90

     I pray let Cassio be receiv'd again.

Oth. Fetch me that handkerchief ; my mind misgives.

Des. Come, come ;

     You 'll never meet a more sufficient man.

Oth. The handkerchief !

[*Des.*   I pray, talk me of Cassio.

Oth. The handkerchief !]

Des.   A man that all his time

     Hath founded his good fortunes on your love,

     Shared dangers with you,—

Oth. The handkerchief !

Des. I' faith, you are to blame.

Oth. Zounds !   *Exit*

Em. Is not this man jealous ?

Des. I ne'er saw this before.
  Sure there 's some wonder in this handkerchief :
  I am most unhappy in the loss of it.

Em. 'Tis not a year or two shows us a man :
  They are all but stomachs, and we all but food ;
  They eat us hungerly, and when they are full
  They belch us.   Look you, Cassio and my husband.

  Enter Cassio and Iago

Iago. There is no other way ; 'tis she must do it :   110
  And, lo, the happiness ! go and importune her.

Des. How now, good Cassio, what 's the news with you ?

Cas. Madam, my former suit : I do beseech you
  That by your virtuous means I may again
  Exist, and be a member of his love,
  Whom I with all the duty of my heart
  Entirely honour : I would not be delay'd.
  If my offence be of such mortal kind,
  That neither service past nor present sorrows
  Nor purpos'd merit in futurity   120
  Can ransom me into his love again,
  But to know so must be my benefit ;
  So shall I clothe me in a forc'd content

And shut myself up in some other course   †
To fortune's alms.

Des.   Alas, thrice-gentle Cassio !
My advocation is not now in tune ;
My lord is not my lord, nor should I know him
Were he in favour as in humour alter'd.
So help me every spirit sanctified,
As I have spoken for you, all my best,   130
And stood within the blank of his displeasure
For my free speech !   You must awhile be patient :
What I can do I will, and more I will
Than for myself I dare ; let that suffice you.

Iago. Is my lord angry ?

Em.   He went hence but now,
And certainly in strange unquietness.

Iago. Can he be angry ?   I have seen the cannon,
When it hath blown his ranks into the air,
And, like the devil, from his very arm
Puff'd his own brother ; and can he be angry ?   140
Something of moment then : I will go meet him :
There 's matter in 't indeed, if he be angry.

Des. I prithee, do so.   *Exit Iago*
           Something sure of state,
Either from Venice, or some unhatch'd practice
Made demonstrable here in Cyprus to him,

Hath puddled his clear spirit, and in such cases
Men's natures wrangle with inferior things,
Though great ones are the object.   'Tis even so ;
For let our finger ache, and it indues
Our other healthful members even to that sense   150
Of pain : nay, we must think men are not gods,
Nor of them look for such observances
As fits the bridal.   Beshrew me much, Emilia,
I was (unhandsome warrior as I am)
Arraigning his unkindness with my soul ;
But now I find I had suborn'd the witness,
And he 's indicted falsely.

Em. Pray heaven it be state-matters, as you think,
And no conception, nor no jealous toy
Concerning you.   160

Des. Alas the day, I never gave him cause !

Em. But jealous souls will not be answer'd so ;
They are not ever jealous for the cause,
But jealous for they are jealous : 'tis a monster
Begot upon itself, born on itself.

Des. Heaven keep that monster from Othello's mind !

Em. Lady, amen.

Des. I will go seek him, Cassio, walk hereabout :
If I do find him fit, I 'll move your suit,
And seek to effect it to my uttermost.   170

Cas. I humbly thank your ladyship.

> *Exeunt Desdemona and Emilia*
> *Enter Bianca*

Bia. Save you, friend Cassio !

Cas.   What make you from home ?
    How is it with you, my most fair Bianca ?
    I' faith, sweet love, I was coming to your house.

Bia. And I was going to your lodging, Cassio.
    What, keep a week away ? seven days and nights ?
    Eight score eight hours, and lovers' absent hours,
    More tedious than the dial, eight score times ?
    O weary reckoning !

Cas.   Pardon me, Bianca,
    I have this while with leaden thoughts been press'd ;   180
    But I shall in a more convenient time
    Strike off this score of absence.   Sweet Bianca,

> *Giving her Desdemona's handkerchief*

    Take me this work out.

Bia.   O Cassio, whence came this ?
    This is some token from a newer friend :
    To the felt absence now I feel a cause :
    Is 't come to this ?   {Well, well.}

Cas.   Go to, woman !
    Throw your vile guesses in the devil's teeth,
    From whence you have them ; you are jealous now

That this is from some mistress, some remembrance :
No, by my faith, Bianca.

Bia.   Why, whose is it ?   190

Cas. I know not, sweet : I found it in my chamber,
I like the work well, ere it be demanded,
As like enough it will, I 'ld have it copied :
Take it, and do 't, and leave me for this time.

Bia. Leave you ? wherefore ?

Cas. I do attend here on the general ;
And think it no addition, nor my wish,
To have him see me woman'd.

Bia.   Why, I pray you ?

Cas. Not that I love you not.

Bia.   But that you do not love me.
I pray you, bring me on the way a little ;   200
And say if I shall see you soon at night.

Cas. 'Tis but a little way that I can bring you,
For I attend here : but I 'll see you soon.

Bia. 'Tis very good ; I must be circumstanc'd.   *Exeunt*

Act Fourth

SCENE I

Cyprus.   Before the castle

Enter Othello and Iago

Iago. Will you think so ?

Oth.   Think so, Iago !

Iago.   What,
  To kiss in private ?

Oth.   An unauthoriz'd kiss.

Iago. Or to be naked with her friend abed
  An hour, or more, not meaning any harm ?

Oth. Naked abed, Iago, and not mean harm ?
  It is hypocrisy against the devil :
  They that mean virtuously and yet do so,
  The devil their virtue tempts, and they tempt heaven.

Iago. So they do nothing, 'tis a venial slip :
  But if I give my wife a handkerchief—   10

Oth. What then ?

Iago. Why, then, 'tis hers, my lord ; and being hers,
  She may, I think, bestow 't on any man.

Oth. She is protectress of her honour too :

May she give that ?

Iago. Her honour is an essence that 's not seen :
They have it very oft that have it not :
But for the handkerchief—

Oth. By heaven, I would most gladly have forgot it :
Thou said'st (O, it comes o'er my memory,   20
As doth the raven o'er the infected house,
Boding to all) he had my handkerchief.

Iago. Ay, what of that ?

Oth.   That 's not so good now.

Iago.   What,
If I had said I had seen him do you wrong ?
Or heard him say . . . as knaves be such abroad,
Who having, by their own importunate suit,
Or by the voluntary dotage of some mistress,
Convinced or supplied them, cannot choose
But they must blab—

Oth.   Hath he said anything ?

Iago. He hath, my lord, but be you well assur'd,   30
No more than he 'll unswear.

Oth.   What hath he said ?

Iago. Faith, that he did—I know not what he did.

Oth. But what ?

Iago. Lie—

Oth.   With her ?

Iago.　　　　　　With her, on her, what you will.

Oth. Lie with her ! lie on her !—We say lie on her, when
　they belie her.—Lie with her ! 'Zounds, that's
　fulsome ! Handkerchiefs — confession — handker-
　chiefs !—{To confess, and be hanged for his labour ;
　first, to be hanged, and then to confess. I tremble
　at it. Nature would not invest herself in such　　40
　shadowing passion without some instruction. It is
　not words that shakes me thus. Pish ! Noses, ears
　and lips. Is 't possible ?—Confess ?—Handkerchief ?
　-—O devil !}　　　　　　　　　*Falls in a trance*

Iago. Work on,
　My medicine, work ! Thus credulous fools are caught,
　And many worthy and chaste dames, even thus
　All guiltless, meet reproach. What, ho ! my lord !
　My lord, I say ! Othello !

　　　　　　　　Enter Cassio

　　　　　　　　How now, Cassio ?

Cas. What 's the matter ?　　　　　　　　　　50

Iago. My lord is fall'n into an epilepsy,
　This is his second fit, he had one yesterday.

Cas. Rub him about the temples.

Iago.　　　　　　　　[No, forbear,]
　The lethargy must have his quiet course :
　If not, he foams at mouth, and by and by

Breaks out to savage madness.   Look, he stirs :
Do you withdraw yourself a little while,
He will recover straight ; when he is gone,
I would on great occasion speak with you.

Exit Cassio

How is it, general ? have you not hurt your head ?   60

Oth. Dost thou mock me ?

Iago.   I mock you ? no, by heaven.
Would you would bear your fortunes like a man !

Oth. A horned man 's a monster, and a beast.

Iago. There 's many a beast then in a populous city,
And many a civil monster.

Oth. Did he confess ?

Iago.   Good sir, be a man,
Think every bearded fellow that 's but yok'd
May draw with you, there 's millions now alive
That nightly lie in those unproper beds
Which they dare swear peculiar : your case is better.   70
O, 'tis the spite of hell, the fiend's arch-mock,
To lip a wanton in a secure couch,
And to suppose her chaste !   No, let me know,
And knowing what I am, I know what she
        shall be.

Oth. O, thou art wise ; 'tis certain.

Iago.   Stand you awhile apart ;

Confine yourself but in a patient list.
Whilst you were here o'erwhelmed with your grief,
A passion most unsuiting such a man,
Cassio came hither; I shifted him away,
And laid good 'scuse upon your ecstasy;   80
Bade him anon retire and here speak with me;
The which he promis'd.   But encave yourself,
And mark the jeers, the gibes, and notable scorns,
That dwell in every region of his face;
For I will make him tell the tale anew,
Where, how, how oft, how long ago, and when
He has and is again to cope your wife:
I say, but mark his gesture; marry, patience;
Or I shall say you are all in all in spleen,
And nothing of a man.

Oth.   Dost thou hear, Iago?   90
I will be found most cunning in my patience;
But—dost thou hear?—most bloody.

Iago.   That's not amiss;
But yet keep time in all.   Will you withdraw?

                              Othello retires

Now will I question Cassio of Bianca,
A housewife that by selling her desires
Buys herself bread and clothes: it is a creature
That dotes on Cassio; as 'tis the strumpet's plague

To beguile many, and be beguil'd by one.
He, when he hears of her, cannot refrain
From the excess of laughter : here he comes :   100

Re-enter Cassio

As he shall smile, Othello shall go mad,
And his unbookish jealousy must conster
Poor Cassio's smiles, gestures, and light behaviour,
Quite in the wrong.   How do you now, lieutenant ?

Cas. The worser that you give me the addition
Whose want even kills me.

Iago. Ply Desdemona well, and you are sure on 't.
Now, if this suit lay in Bianca's power,
How quickly should you speed !

Cas.   Alas, poor caitiff !

Oth. Look, how he laughs already !   110

Iago. I never knew a woman love man so.

Cas. Alas, poor rogue, I think, i' faith, she loves me.

Oth. Now he denies it faintly, and laughs it out.

Iago. Do you hear, Cassio ?

Oth.   Now he importunes him
To tell it o'er : go to ; well said, well said.

Iago. She gives it out that you shall marry her ;
Do you intend it ?

Cas. Ha, ha, ha !

Oth. Do you triumph, Roman, do you triumph ?

Cas. I marry her? {what, a customer?} I prithee, bear 120
     some charity to my wit; do not think it so unwhole-
     some. Ha, ha, ha!

Oth. So, so, so, so: laugh that wins.

Iago. Faith, the cry goes you shall marry her.

Cas. Prithee, say true.

Iago. I am a very villain else.

Oth. Have you scor'd me? Well.

Cas. This is the monkey's own giving out: she is per-
     suaded I will marry her, out of her own love and
     flattery, not out of my promise. 130

Oth. Iago beckons me; now he begins the story.

Cas. She was here even now, she haunts me in every
     place. I was the other day talking on the sea-bank
     with certain Venetians, and thither comes this bauble,
     by this hand, she falls thus about my neck—

Oth. Crying 'O dear Cassio!' as it were: his gesture
     imports it.

Cas. So hangs, and lolls, and weeps upon me; so hales,
     and pulls me: ha, ha, ha!

Oth. Now he tells how she pluck'd him to my chamber. 140
     I see that nose of yours, but not that dog I shall
     throw 't to.

Cas. Well, I must leave her company.

Iago. Before me! look, where she comes.

Cas. 'Tis such another fitchew! marry, a perfum'd one.

Enter Bianca

   What do you mean by this haunting of me?

Bia. Let the devil and his dam haunt you! What did
   you mean by that same handkerchief you gave me
   even now? I was a fine fool to take it. I must take
   out the work? A likely piece of work, that you   150
   should find it in your chamber, and not know who
   left it there! This is some minx's token, and I must
   take out the work? There; give it your hobby-
   horse: wheresoever you had it, I'll take out no
   work on 't.

Cas. How now, my sweet Bianca, how now, how now?

Oth. By heaven, that should be my handkerchief!

Bia. An you'll come to supper to-night, you may, an
   you will not, come when you are next prepar'd for.

Exit

Iago. After her, after her.   160

Cas. Faith, I must, she 'll rail i' the street else.

Iago. Will you sup there?

Cas. Faith, I intend so.

Iago. Well, I may chance to see you, for I would very fain
   speak with you.

Cas. Prithee, come, will you?

Iago. Go to, say no more.   [*Exit Cassio*]

107

Oth. (*advancing*) How shall I murder him, Iago?

Iago. Did you perceive how he laugh'd at his vice?

Oth. O Iago!   170

Iago. And did you see the handkerchief?

Oth. Was that mine?

Iago. {Yours, by this hand: and to see how he prizes the foolish woman your wife! she gave it him, and he hath given it his whore.}

Oth. I would have him nine years a-killing; a fine woman! a fair woman! a sweet woman!

Iago. Nay, you must forget.

Oth. Ay, let her rot and perish, and be damn'd to-night, for she shall not live: no, my heart is turn'd to   180 stone; I strike it, and it hurts my hand. O, the world has not a sweeter creature; she might lie by an emperor's side, and command him tasks.

Iago. Nay, that's not your way.

Oth. Hang her, I do but say what she is: so delicate with her needle, an admirable musician, O, she will sing the savageness out of a bear: of so high and plenteous wit and invention:—

Iago. She's the worse for all this.

Oth. A thousand thousand times: and then, of so gentle   190 a condition!

Iago. Ay, too gentle.

Oth. Ay, that's certain : but yet the pity of it, Iago !
   {O Iago,} the pity {of it, Iago !}

Iago. If you be so fond over her iniquity, give her patent
   to offend, for, if it touches not you, it comes near
   nobody.

Oth. I will chop her into messes . . . cuckold me !

Iago. O, 'tis foul in her.

Oth. With mine officer !   200

Iago. That's fouler.

Oth. Get me some poison, Iago, this night. I'll not
   expostulate with her, lest her body and beauty un-
   provide my mind again : this night, Iago.

Iago. Do it not with poison, strangle her in her bed, even
   the bed she hath contaminated.

Oth. Good, good, the justice of it pleases, very good.

Iago. And for Cassio, let me be his undertaker : you shall
   hear more by midnight.   [*A trumpet within*]

Oth. Excellent good.   What trumpet is that same ?   210

Iago. Something from Venice, sure. 'Tis Lodovico
   Come from the duke : and, see, your wife is with him.

   Enter Lodovico, Desdemona, and Attendants

Lod. God save the worthy general !

Oth.   With all my heart, sir.

Lod. The duke and senators of Venice greet you.

                                   Gives him a letter

Oth. I kiss the instrument of their pleasures.

                         Opens the letter, and reads

Des. And what's the news, good cousin Lodovico?

Iago. I am very glad to see you, signior; . . .
    Welcome to Cyprus.

Lod. I thank you.   How does Lieutenant Cassio?

Iago. Lives, sir.   220

Des. Cousin, there's fall'n between him and my lord
    An unkind breach, but you shall make all well.

Oth. Are you sure of that?

Des. My lord?

Oth. (*reads*) 'This fail you not to do, as you will . . .'

Lod. He did not call, he's busy in the paper.
    Is there division between thy lord and Cassio?

Des. A most unhappy one; I would do much
    To atone them, for the love I bear to Cassio.

Oth. Fire and brimstone!

Des.   My lord?

Oth.   Are you wise?   230

Des. What, is he angry?

Lod.   May be the letter mov'd him;
    For, as I think, they do command him home,
    Deputing Cassio in his government.

Des. By my troth, I am glad on 't.

Oth.   Indeed!

Des.   My lord ?

Oth. I am glad to see you mad.   †

Des.   How, sweet Othello ?

Oth. Devil !   *Striking her*

Des. I have not deserv'd this.

Lod. My lord, this would not be believ'd in Venice,
  Though I should swear I saw 't : 'tis very much :
  Make her amends, she weeps.

Oth.   O devil, devil !   240
  If that the earth could teem with women's tears,
  Each drop she falls would prove a crocodile.
  Out of my sight !

Des.   I will not stay to offend you. *Going*

Lod. Truly, an obedient lady :
  I do beseech your lordship, call her back.

Oth. Mistress !

Des. My lord ?

Oth. What would you with her, sir ?

Lod.   Who, I, my lord ?

Oth. Ay ; you did wish that I would make her turn :
  Sir, she can turn, and turn, and yet go on,   250
  And turn again, and she can weep, sir, weep ;
  And she 's obedient, as you say, obedient ;
  Very obedient, proceed you in your tears.
  Concerning this, sir,—O well-painted passion !

I am commanded here : . . . get you away,
I 'll send for you anon : . . . Sir, I obey the mandate,
And will return to Venice : . . . hence, avaunt !

Exit Desdemona

Cassio shall have my place ; and, sir, to-night,
I do entreat that we may sup together,
You are welcome, sir, to Cyprus : . . . goats and
monkeys ! *Exit* 26c

Lod. Is this the noble Moor whom our full senate
Call all in all sufficient ? This the noble nature
Whom passion could not shake ? whose solid virtue
The shot of accident nor dart of chance
Could neither graze nor pierce ?

Iago. He is much chang'd.

Lod. Are his wits safe ? is he not light of brain ?

Iago. He 's that he is, I may not breathe my censure
What he might be, if as he might he is not,
I would to heaven he were !

Lod. What, strike his wife.

Iago. Faith, that was not so well ; yet would I knew 270
That stroke would prove the worst !

Lod. Is it his use ?
Or did the letters work upon his blood,
And new create this fault ?

Iago. Alas, alas !

It is not honesty in me to speak
What I have seen and known ; you shall observe him,
And his own courses will denote him so
That I may save my speech : do but go after,
And mark how he continues.

Lod. I am sorry that I am deceiv'd in him.   *Exeunt*

SCENE II

A room in the castle

Enter Othello and Emilia

Oth. You have seen nothing, then ?

Em. Nor ever heard, nor ever did suspect.

Oth. Yes, and you have seen Cassio and she together.

Em. But then I saw no harm, and then I heard
Each syllable that breath made up between them.

Oth. What, did they never whisper ?

Em.   Never, my lord.

Oth. Nor send you out o' the way ?

Em. Never.

Oth. To fetch her fan, her gloves, her mask, nor nothing ?

Em. Never, my lord.   10

Oth. That 's strange.

Em. I durst, my lord, to wager she is honest,

Lay down my soul at stake : if you think other,
Remove your thought, it doth abuse your bosom.
If any wretch have put this in your head,
Let heaven requite it with the serpent's curse,
For if she be not honest, chaste, and true,
There's no man happy ; the purest of her sex
Is foul as slander.

Oth.   Bid her come hither : go.   *Exit Emilia*   20
She says enough, yet she's a simple bawd
That cannot say as much.   This is a subtle whore,
A closet, lock and key, of villanous secrets,
And yet she'll kneel and pray, I have seen her do't.

Enter Desdemona with Emilia

Des. My lord, what is your will ?

Oth.   Pray, chuck, come hither.

Des. What is your pleasure ?

Oth.   Let me see your eyes . . .
Look in my face.

Des.   What horrible fancy's this ?

Oth. (*to Emilia*) Some of your function, mistress,
Leave procreants alone, and shut the door,
Cough, or cry hem, if any body come,
Your mystery, your mystery : nay, dispatch.   30

Exit Emilia

Des. Upon my knees, what doth your speech import ?

I understand a fury in your words,
[But not the words.]

Oth. Why, what art thou ?

Des. Your wife, my lord, your true and loyal wife.

Oth. Come, swear it, damn thyself,
Lest, being like one of heaven, the devils themselves
Should fear to seize thee : therefore be double-damn'd ;
Swear thou art honest.

Des.   Heaven doth truly know it.

Oth. Heaven truly knows, that thou art false as hell.   40

Des. To whom, my lord, with whom ? how am I false ?

Oth. O Desdemona !   Away ! away ! away !

Des. Alas the heavy day !   Why do you weep ?
Am I the occasion of those tears, my lord ?
If haply you my father do suspect
An instrument of this your calling back,
Lay not your blame on me : if you have lost him,
Why, I have lost him too.

Oth.   Had it pleas'd heaven
To try me with affliction, had they rain'd
All kinds of sores and shames on my bare head,   50
Steep'd me in poverty, to the very lips,
Given to captivity me and my {utmost} hopes,
I should have found in some part of my soul
A drop of patience : but, alas, to make me

A fixed figure for the time of scorn   †
To point his slow unmoving fingers at . . . oh, oh !
Yet could I bear that too, well, very well :
But there ; where I have garner'd up my heart,
Where either I must live or bear no life,
The fountain from the which my current runs,   60
Or else dries up, to be discarded thence !
Or keep it as a cistern for foul toads
To knot and gender in !   Turn thy complexion there, †
Patience, thou young and rose-lipp'd cherubin,
I here look grim as hell !

Des. I hope my noble lord esteems me honest.

Oth. O, ay, as summer flies, are in the shambles,
That quicken even with blowing.
O thou black weed, why art so lovely fair ?
Thou smell'st so sweet that the sense aches at thee ;   70
Would thou hadst ne'er been born !

Des. Alas, what ignorant sin have I committed ?

Oth. Was this fair paper, this most goodly book,
Made to write ' whore ' on ? . . . What committed ?
{Committed !   O thou public commoner !
I should make very forges of my cheeks,
That would to cinders burn up modesty,
Did I but speak thy deeds.   What committed ?}
Heaven stops the nose at it, and the moon winks,

The bawdy wind, that kisses all it meets,   80
Is hush'd within the hollow mine of earth,
And will not hear 't . . . what committed ?
Impudent strumpet !

Des.   By heaven, you do me wrong.

Oth. Are not you a strumpet ?

Des.   No, as I am a Christian :
If to preserve this vessel for my lord
From any hated foul unlawful touch
Be not to be a strumpet, I am none.

Oth. What, not a whore ?

Des.   No, as I shall be sav'd.

Oth. Is 't possible ?

Des. O, heaven, forgiveness !

Oth.   I cry you mercy then :   90
I took you for that cunning whore of Venice
That married with Othello.   (*raising his voice*) You,
        mistress,
That have the office opposite to Saint Peter,
And keeps the gates in hell !

                    Re-enter Emilia

                    Ay, you, you, you !
We have done our course ; there 's money for your
        pains,
I pray you, turn the key, and keep our counsel.   *Exit*

117

Em. Alas, what does this gentleman conceive?
　　How do you, madam? how do you, my good lady?
Des. Faith, half asleep.
Em. Good madam, what's the matter with my lord?　　100
Des. With who?
Em. Why, with my lord, madam.
{*Des.* Who is thy lord?
Em. 　　　　　　He that is yours, sweet lady.}
Des. I have none: do not talk to me, Emilia;
　　I cannot weep, nor answer have I none
　　But what should go by water.　Prithee, to-night
　　Lay on my bed my wedding sheets, remember,
　　And call thy husband hither.
Em. 　　　　　　　Here is a change indeed!

　　　　　　　　　　　　　　　　　Exit

Des. 'Tis meet I should be us'd so, very meet.
　　How have I been behav'd, that he might stick　　110
　　The small'st opinion on my greatest abuse?　　†

　　　　　Re-enter Emilia, with Iago

Iago. What is your pleasure, madam?　How is 't with you?
Des. I cannot tell: those that do teach young babes
　　Do it with gentle means, and easy tasks:
　　He might have chid me so, for, in good faith,
　　I am a child at chiding.
Iago. 　　　　　　What is the matter, lady?

Em. Alas, Iago, my lord hath so bewhor'd her,
  Thrown such despite, and heavy terms upon her,
  As true hearts cannot bear.

Des. Am I that name, Iago ?

Iago.   What name, fair lady ?   120

Des. Such as she says my lord did say I was.

Em. He call'd her whore : a beggar in his drink
  Could not have laid such terms upon his callet.

Iago. Why did he so ?

Des. I do not know : I am sure I am none such.

Iago. Do not weep, do not weep.   Alas the day !

Em. Hath she forsook so many noble matches,
  Her father, and her country, and her friends,
  To be call'd whore ? would it not make one weep ?

Des. It is my wretched fortune.

Iago.   Beshrew him for 't !   130
  How comes this trick upon him ?

Des.   Nay, heaven doth know.

Em. I will be hang'd, if some eternal villain,
  Some busy and insinuating rogue,
  Some cogging, cozening slave, to get some office,
  Have not devised this slander, I 'll be hang'd else.

Iago. Fie, there is no such man, it is impossible.

Des. If any such there be, heaven pardon him !

Em. A halter pardon him, and hell gnaw his bones !

Why should he call her whore? who keeps her
    company?
What place? what time? what form? what likeli-
    hood? 140
The Moor's abus'd by some outrageous knave,
Some base notorious knave, some scurvy fellow.
O heaven, that such companions thou 'ldst unfold,
And put in every honest hand a whip
To lash the rascal naked through the world,
Even from the east to the west!

Iago.   Speak within doors.

Em. O, fie upon him! Some such squire he was
That turn'd your wit, the seamy side without,
And made you to suspect me with the Moor.

Iago. You are a fool, go to.

Des.   O good Iago,   †
What shall I do to win my lord again? 151
Good friend, go to him, for, by this light of heaven,
I know not how I lost him. {Here I kneel:
If e'er my will did trespass 'gainst his love
Either in discourse of thought or actual deed,
Or that mine eyes, mine ears, or any sense,
Delighted them in any other form,
Or that I do not yet, and ever did,
And ever will, though he do shake me off

To beggarly divorcement, love him dearly,   160
Comfort forswear me !   Unkindness may do much ;
And his unkindness may defeat my life,
But never taint my love.   I cannot say ' whore ' :
It doth abhor me now I speak the word ;
To do the act that might the addition earn
Not the world's mass of vanity could make me.}

Iago. I pray you, be content, 'tis but his humour ;
The business of the state does him offence,
[And he does chide with you.]

Des. If 'twere no other,—

Iago.   'Tis but so, I warrant you. *Trumpets within* 170
Hark, how these instruments summon you to
        supper !
And the great messengers of Venice stay :   †
Go in, and weep not ; all things shall be well.

                    Exeunt Desdemona and Emilia
                    Enter Roderigo

How now, Roderigo ?

Rod. I do not find that thou deal'st justly with me.

Iago. What in the contrary ?

Rod. Every day thou doffest me with some device, Iago ;
    and rather, as it seems to me, thou keepest from me
    all conveniency than suppliest me with the least
    advantage of hope.   I will indeed no longer endure 180

it, nor am I yet persuaded to put up in peace what
already I have foolishly suffered.

Iago. Will you hear me, Roderigo ?

Rod. Faith, I have heard too much ; for your words and
performance are no kin together.

Iago. You charge me most unjustly.

Rod. {With nought but truth.} I have wasted myself
out of means. The jewels you have had from me,
to deliver to Desdemona, would half have corrupted
a votarist : you have told me she hath received them, 190
and returned me expectation and comforts, of sudden respect and acquaintance ; but I find none.

Iago. Well ; go to ; very well.

Rod. Very well ? go to ? I cannot go to, man, it is not
very well ; by this hand, I say 'tis very scurvy, and
begin to find myself fopp'd in it.

Iago. Very well.

Rod. I say it is not very well. I will make myself known
to Desdemona ; if she will return me my jewels, I
will give over my suit, and repent my unlawful 200
solicitation ; if not, assure yourself I 'll seek satisfaction of you.

Iago. You have said now.

Rod. Ay, and I have said nothing but what I protest intend-
ment of doing.

Iago. Why, now I see there 's mettle in thee, and even from
this time do build on thee a better opinion than ever
before ; give me thy hand, Roderigo : thou hast
taken against me a most just exception, but yet, I
protest, I have dealt most directly in thy affairs.   210

Rod. It hath not appear'd.

Iago. I grant indeed it hath not appear'd, and your suspicion is not without wit and judgement.   But,
Roderigo, if thou hast that within thee indeed, which
I have greater reason to believe now than ever, I
mean purpose, courage, and valour, this night show
it : if thou the next night following enjoyest not
Desdemona, take me from this world with treachery,
and devise engines for my life.

Rod. Well, {what is it} ? is it within reason and com-   220
pass ?

Iago. Sir, there is especial command come from Venice to
depute Cassio in Othello's place.

Rod. Is that true ? why then Othello and Desdemona
return again to Venice.

Iago. O, no, he goes into Mauritania, and takes away with
him the fair Desdemona, unless his abode be linger'd
here by some accident, wherein none can be so
determinate as the removing of Cassio.

Rod. How do you mean, removing of him ?   230

Iago. Why, by making him uncapable of Othello's place,
    knocking out his brains.

Rod. And that you would have me to do.

Iago. Ay, an if you dare do yourself a profit and a right.
    He sups to-night with a harlot, and thither will I go
    to him : . . . he knows not yet of his honourable
    fortune. If you will watch his going thence, which
    I will fashion to fall out between twelve and one, you
    may take him at your pleasure : I will be near to
    second your attempt, and he shall fall between us : 240
    come, stand not amazed at it, but go along with me,
    I will show you such a necessity in his death that you
    shall think yourself bound to put it on him. It is
    now high supper-time, and the night grows to
    waste : about it.

Rod. I will hear further reason for this.

Iago. And you shall be satisfied.   *Exeunt*

SCENE III

Another room in the castle

*Enter Othello, Lodovico, Desdemona, Emilia, and
Attendants*

Lod. I do beseech you, sir, trouble yourself no further.

Oth. O, pardon me ; it shall do me good to walk.

Lod. Madam, good night, I humbly thank your ladyship.

Des. Your honour is most welcome.

Oth.   Will you walk, sir ? . . .

O Desdemona.

Des. My lord ?

Oth. Get you to bed, on the instant I will be return'd,
forthwith, dispatch your attendant there, . . . look
it be done.

Des. I will, my lord.   10

Exeunt Othello, Lodovico, and Attendants

Em. How goes it now ? he looks gentler than he did.

Des. He says he will return incontinent :

He hath commanded me to go to bed,

And bade me to dismiss you.

Em.   Dismiss me ?

Des. It was his bidding, therefore, good Emilia,

Give me my nightly wearing, and adieu :

We must not now displease him.

Em. I would you had never seen him !

Des. So would not I, my love doth so approve him,

That even his stubbornness, his checks and frowns   20

(Prithee, unpin me) have grace and favour in them.

Em. I have laid those sheets you bade me on the bed.

Des. All 's one, good faith ; how foolish are our minds !

If I do die before thee, prithee, shroud me

In one of those same sheets.

Em.   Come, come, you talk.

Des. My mother had a maid call'd Barbara :
 She was in love, and he she lov'd prov'd mad
 And did forsake her : she had a song of ' willow ; '
 An old thing 'twas, but it express'd her fortune,
 And she died singing it : that song to-night   30
 Will not go from my mind ; {I have much to do
 But to go hang my head all at one side
 And sing it like poor Barbara.   Prithee, dispatch.

Em. Shall I go fetch your night-gown ?

Des.   No, unpin me here.
 This Lodovico is a proper man.

Em. A very handsome man.

Des. He speaks well.

Em. I know a lady in Venice would have walked barefoot
 to Palestine for a touch of his nether lip.

Des. (*singing*) The poor soul sat sighing by a sycamore
     tree,   40
    Sing all a green willow ;
 Her hand on her bosom, her head on her knee,
    Sing willow, willow, willow :
 The fresh streams ran by her, and murmur'd her
     moans ;
    Sing willow, willow, willow ;

Her salt tears fell from her, which soften'd the stones ;—
     Sing willow,

(Lay by these)

(*singing*) Willow, willow,

(Prithee, hie thee ; he 'll come anon)   50

(*singing*) Sing all a green willow must be my garland.
     Let nobody blame him ; his scorn I approve,—

Nay, that 's not next.}   Hark ! who 's that knocks ?

Em. It is the wind.

Des. {(*singing*) I call'd my love false love ; but what said
     he then ?
     Sing willow, willow, willow :
If I court moe women, you 'll couch with moe men.}

Now get thee gone ; good night.   Mine eyes do itch ;
Doth that bode weeping ?

Em.   'Tis neither here nor there.

{*Des.* I have heard it said so. O, these men, these men ! 60
Dost thou in conscience think,—tell me, Emilia,—
That there be women do abuse their husbands
In such gross kind ?

Em.   There be some such, no question.}

Des. Wouldst thou do such a deed, for all the world ?

Em. Why, would not you ?

Des.   No, by this heavenly light !

Em. Nor I neither, by this heavenly light, I might do it
as well in the dark.

Des. Wouldst thou do such a thing for all the world ?

Em. The world is a huge thing : it is a great price
For a small vice.

Des.   Good troth, I think thou wouldst not. 70

Em. By my troth, I think I should, and undo 't when I had
done it.   Marry, I would not do such a thing for a
joint-ring, or for measures of lawn, nor for gowns,
or petticoats, nor caps, nor any such exhibition ; but,
for the whole world ? 'uds pity, who would not
make her husband a cuckold to make him a monarch ?
I should venture purgatory for it.

Des. Beshrew me, if I would do such a wrong
For the whole world.

Em. Why, the wrong is but a wrong i' the world ; and   80
having the world for your labour, 'tis a wrong in your
own world, and you might quickly make it right.

Des. I do not think there is any such woman.

Em. Yes, a dozen, and as many to the vantage as would
store the world they play'd for.
{But I do think it is their husbands' faults
If wives do fall : say that they slack their duties
And pour our treasures into foreign laps,

Or else break out in peevish jealousies,
Throwing restraint upon us ; or say they strike us,   90
Or scant our former having in despite,
Why, we have galls, and though we have some grace,
Yet have we some revenge.   Let husbands know
Their wives have sense like them : they see, and smell,
And have their palates both for sweet and sour,
As husbands have : what is it that they do,
When they change us for others ?   Is it sport ?
I think it is : and doth affection breed it ?
I think it doth : is 't frailty that thus errs ?
It is so too : and have not we affections ?   100
Desires for sport ? and frailty, as men have ?
Then let 'em use us well : else let 'em know,
The ills we do, their ills instruct us so.}

Des. Good night, good night : heaven me such uses send,
Not to pick bad from bad, but by bad mend !

Exeunt

Act Fifth

Cyprus.   A street

Enter Iago and Roderigo

Iago. Here, stand behind this bulk, straight will he come,
 Wear thy good rapier bare, and put it home,
 Quick, quick, fear nothing, I 'll be at thy elbow :
 It makes us or it mars us, think of that,
 And fix most firm thy resolution.

Rod. Be near at hand, I may miscarry in 't.

Iago. Here, at thy hand, be bold, and take thy sword.

           Retires

Rod. I have no great devotion to the deed ;
 And yet he hath given me satisfying reasons :
 'Tis but a man gone.   Forth, my sword, he dies. 10

Iago. I have rubb'd this young quat almost to the sense,
 And he grows angry.   Now, whether he kill Cassio,
 Or Cassio him, or each do kill the other,
 Every way makes my gain : live Roderigo,   †
 He calls me to a restitution large
 Of gold and jewels, that I bobb'd from him,

As gifts to Desdemona :
It must not be : if Cassio do remain,
He has a daily beauty in his life
That makes me ugly ; and besides, the Moor   20
May unfold me to him ; there stand I in peril :
No, he must die ; be 't so ; I hear him coming.

Enter Cassio

Rod. I know his gait, 'tis he, villain, thou diest !

Makes a pass at Cassio

Cas. That thrust had been mine enemy indeed,
But that my coat is better than thou think'st :
I will make proof of thine.

Draws, and wounds Roderigo

Rod.   O, I am slain !

Iago from behind wounds Cassio in the leg, and exit

Cas. I am maim'd for ever. Light, ho ! murder ! murder !

Falls

Enter Othello

Oth. The voice of Cassio, Iago keeps his word.

Rod. O, villain that I am !

Oth.   Hark, 'tis even so.

Cas. O, help, ho ! light ! a surgeon !   30

Oth. 'Tis he, O brave Iago, honest and just,
That hast such noble sense of thy friend's wrong.
Thou teachest me ; . . . minion, your dear lies dead,

And your fate hies apace : strumpet, I come !

Forth of my heart those charms, thine eyes, are
    blotted :

Thy bed lust-stain'd shall with lust's blood be spotted.

                          Exit

Enter Lodovico and Gratiano

Cas. What, ho ! no watch ? no passage ? murder ! murder !

Gra. 'Tis some mischance, the cry is very direful.

Cas. O, help !

Lod. Hark !   40

Rod. O wretched villain.

Lod. Two or three groan : it is a heavy night :

These may be counterfeits, let 's think 't unsafe

To come into the cry without more help.

Rod. Nobody come ? then shall I bleed to death.

Lod. Hark !

Re-enter Iago, [*with a light*]

Gra. Here 's one comes in his shirt, with light and weapons.

Iago. Who 's there ? whose noise is this that cries on
    murder ?

Lod. I do not know.

Iago.   Did not you hear a cry ?

Cas. Here, here ! for heaven's sake, help me !

Iago.   What 's the matter ? 50

Gra. This is Othello's ancient, as I take it.

Lod. The same indeed, a very valiant fellow.

Iago. What are you here that cry so grievously ?

Cas. Iago, O, I am spoil'd, undone by villains !
　　Give me some help.

Iago. O me, lieutenant ! what villains have done this ?

Cas. I think the one of them is hereabout,
　　And cannot make away.

Iago.　　　　　　　　O treacherous villains :
　　What are you there ? come in and give some help.
　　　　　　　　　　　To Lodovico and Gratiano

Rod. O, help me here !　　　　　　　　　　　　　60

Cas. That 's one of them.

Iago.　　　　　　　　O murderous slave!   O villain !
　　　　　　　　　　　　Stabs Roderigo

Rod. O damn'd Iago !   O inhuman dog ! . . . oh, oh, oh !

Iago. Kill him i' the dark !   Where be those bloody thieves ?
　　How silent is this town !   Ho ! murder ! murder !
　　What may you be ? are you of good or evil ?

Lod. As you shall prove us, praise us.

Iago. Signior Lodovico ?

Lod. He, sir.

Iago. I cry you mercy.   Here 's Cassio hurt by villains.

Gra. Cassio ?　　　　　　　　　　　　　　　70

Iago. How is it, brother ?

Cas. My leg is cut in two.

Iago.   Marry, heaven forbid !
    Light, gentlemen, I 'll bind it with my shirt.
                    Enter Bianca

Bia. What is the matter, ho ? who is 't that cried ?

Iago. Who is 't that cried ?

Bia. O my dear Cassio ! O my sweet Cassio ! {O
    Cassio,} Cassio, Cassio !

Iago. O notable strumpet ! Cassio, may you suspect
    Who they should be that thus have mangled you ?

Cas. No.   80

Gra. I am sorry to find you thus : I have been to seek you

{*Iago.* Lend me a garter. So. O, for a chair,
    To bear him easily hence !}

Bia. Alas, he faints ! O Cassio, Cassio, Cassio !

Iago. Gentlemen all, I do suspect this trash
    To bear a part in this.   †
    Patience awhile, good Cassio. {Come, come ;}
    Lend me a light. Know we this face or no ?
    Alas, my friend, and my dear countryman ;
    Roderigo ? no :—yes, sure : O heaven ! Roderigo.   90

Gra. What, of Venice ?

Iago. Even he, sir, did you know him ?

Gra.   Know him ? ay.

Iago. Signior Gratiano ? I cry you gentle pardon ;
    These bloody accidents must excuse my manners,

That so neglected you.

Gra.   I am glad to see you.

Iago. How do you, Cassio ?   O, a chair, a chair.

Gra. Roderigo !

Iago. He, 'tis he. (*A chair brought in.*)   O, that 's well
      said ; the chair :

Some good man bear him carefully from hence ;

I 'll fetch the general's surgeon. (*to Bia.*) For you,
      mistress,   100

Save you your labour.   He that lies slain here, Cassio,

Was my dear friend : what malice was between you ?

Cas. None in the world ; nor do I know the man.

Iago. (*to Bia.*) What, look you pale ? O, bear him out o'
      the air.   *Cassio and Roderigo are borne off*

Stay you, good gentlemen.   Look you pale, mistress ? †

Do you perceive the gestures of her eye ?

Nay, if you stir, we shall have more anon.

Behold her well I pray you, look upon her,

Do you see, gentlemen ? nay, guiltiness will speak,

Though tongues were out of use.   110

Enter Emilia

Em. 'Las, what 's the matter ? what 's the matter, husband ?

Iago. Cassio has here been set on in the dark,

By Roderigo, and fellows that are 'scap'd :

He 's almost slain, and Roderigo dead.   †

Em. Alas, good gentleman, alas, good Cassio !

Iago. This is the fruit of whoring ; pray, Emilia,
    Go know of Cassio where he supp'd to-night.
    What, do you shake at that ?

Bia. He supp'd at my house, but I therefore shake not.

Iago. O, did he so ? I charge you, go with me.   120

Em. Fie, fie upon thee, strumpet !

Bia. I am no strumpet, but of life as honest
    As you that thus abuse me.

Em.   As I ! faugh ! fie upon thee !

Iago. Kind gentlemen, let 's go see poor Cassio dress'd.
    Come, mistress, you must tell 's another tale.
    Emilia, run you to the citadel,
    And tell my lord and lady what hath happ'd !
    Will you go on, I pray.   *(aside)* This is the night
    That either makes me or fordoes me quite.   *Exeunt*

SCENE II

A bedchamber in the castle : {Desdemona in bed asleep}

Enter Othello [with a light]

Oth. It is the cause, it is the cause, my soul,
    Let me not name it to you, you chaste stars !
    It is the cause, yet I 'll not shed her blood,

Nor scar that whiter skin of hers than snow,
And smooth as monumental alabaster ;
Yet she must die, else she 'll betray more men.
Put out the light, and then put out the light :
If I quench thee, thou flaming minister,
I can again thy former light restore,
Should I repent me : but once put out thine,   10
Thou cunning pattern of excelling nature,
I know not where is that Promethean heat
That can thy light relume.   When I have pluck'd the
    rose,
I cannot give it vital growth again,
It must needs wither : I 'll smell it on the tree.

                                   [Kisses her]

A balmy breath, that doth almost persuade
Justice herself to break her sword !   Once more :
Be thus, when thou art dead, and I will kill thee,
And love thee after : once more, and this the last :
So sweet was ne'er so fatal.   I must weep,   20
But they are cruel tears : this sorrow 's heavenly ;
It strikes where it doth love : she wakes.

Des. Who 's there ?   Othello ?
Oth.   Ay, Desdemona.
Des. Will you come to bed, my lord ?
Oth. Have you pray'd to-night, Desdemona ?

Des. Ay, my lord.

Oth. If you bethink yourself of any crime
    Unreconcil'd as yet to heaven and grace,
    Solicit for it straight.

Des. Alas, my lord, what may you mean by that?   30

Oth. Well, do it, and be brief, I will walk by:
    I would not kill thy unprepared spirit;
    No, heaven forfend! I would not kill thy soul.

Des. Talk you of killing?

Oth. Ay, I do.

Des. Then heaven have mercy on me!

Oth. Amen, with all my heart!

Des. If you say so, I hope you will not kill me.

Oth. Hum!

Des. And yet I fear you, for you are fatal then   40
    When your eyes roll so: why I should fear I know not,
    Since guiltiness I know not, but yet I feel I fear.

Oth. Think on thy sins.

Des.   They are loves I bear to you.

Oth. And for that thou diest.

Des. That death's unnatural that kills for loving.
    Alas, why gnaw you so your nether lip?
    Some bloody passion shakes your very frame:
    These are portents; but yet I hope, {I hope,}
    They do not point on me.

Oth.   Peace, and be still !

Des. I will, so ; what 's the matter ?   50

Oth. That handkerchief which I so lov'd and gave thee
       Thou gavest to Cassio.

Des.   No, by my life and soul !
       Send for the man, and ask him.

Oth.   Sweet soul, take heed,
       Take heed of perjury ; thou art on thy death-bed.

Des. Ay, but not yet to die.

Oth.   Yes, presently :
       Therefore confess thee freely of thy sin ;
       For to deny each article with oath
       Cannot remove nor choke the strong conceit
       That I do groan withal.   Thou art to die.

Des. Then Lord have mercy on me !

Oth.   I say, amen.   60

Des. And have you mercy too !
       I never did offend you in my life, . . .
       Never lov'd Cassio,
       But with such general warranty of heaven
       As I might love : I never gave him token.

Oth. By heaven, I saw my handkerchief in his hand.
       O perjur'd woman ! thou dost stone my heart,
       And makest me call what I intend to do
       A murder, which I thought a sacrifice :

I saw the handkerchief.

Des. He found it then,   70
I naver gave it him, send for him hither,
Let him confess a truth.

Oth.   He has confess'd.

Des. What, my lord?

Oth. That he hath . . . us'd thee.   †

Des.   How? unlawfully?

Oth. Ay.

Des. He will not say so.

Oth.   No, his mouth is stopp'd;
Honest Iago hath ta'en order for 't.

Des. My fear interprets then . . . what, is he dead?

Oth. Had all his hairs been lives, my great revenge
Had stomach for them all.   80

Des. Alas, he is betray'd, and I undone!

Oth. O strumpet! . . . weep'st thou for him to my face?

Des. O, banish me, my lord, but kill me not!

Oth. Down, strumpet!

Des. Kill me to-morrow, let me live to-night!

Oth. Nay, an you strive,—

Des. But half an hour!

{*Oth.*   Being done, there is no pause.

Des.} But while I say one prayer!

Oth.   It is too late.   *He stifles her*

[Des. O Lord, Lord, Lord !]

Em. (within) My lord, my lord ! what, ho ! my lord, my
        lord !   90

Oth. What voice is this ?   Not dead ? not yet quite dead ?
    I that am cruel am yet merciful,
    I would not have thee linger in thy pain, . . .
    So, so.

Em. (within) What, ho ! my lord, my lord !

Oth.   Who 's there ?

Em. (within) O, good my lord, I 'ld speak a word with you !

Oth. Yes, 'tis Emilia, by and by : she 's dead :
    'Tis like she comes to speak of Cassio's death.
    The noise was here.   Ha ! no more moving ?
    Still as the grave.   Shall she come in ? were 't good ? 100
    I think she stirs again ; no, what 's the best ?
    If she come in, she 'll sure speak to my wife :
    My wife, my wife, my wife ?   I have no wife.
    O, insupportable !   O heavy hour !
    Methinks it should be now a huge eclipse
    Of sun and moon, and that the affrighted globe
    Should yawn at alteration.

Em. (within) I do beseech you I may speak with you,
    Good my lord !

Oth. I had forgot thee : O, come in, Emilia.   110
    Soft, by and by.   Let me the curtains draw.

    Where art thou ?   *Unlocks the door*

                Enter Emilia

                What 's the matter with thee now ?

Em. O, my good lord, yonder 's foul murders done !

Oth. What, now ?

Em. But now, my lord.

Oth. It is the very error of the moon ;
    She comes more near the earth than she was wont
    And makes men mad.

Em. Cassio, my lord, hath kill'd a young Venetian
    Call'd Roderigo.

Oth.   Roderigo kill'd ?   120
    And Cassio kill'd ?

Em.   No, Cassio is not kill'd.

Oth. Not Cassio kill'd ? then murder 's out of tune,
    And sweet revenge grows harsh.

Des. O, falsely, falsely murder'd !

Em.   O Lord, what cry is that ?

Oth. That ? what ?

Em. Out, and alas, it is my lady's voice.
    Help, help, ho, help !   O lady, speak again !
    Sweet Desdemona, O sweet mistress, speak !

Des. A guiltless death I die.

Em. O, who has done this deed ?   130

Des. Nobody, I myself, farewell :

Commend me to my kind lord, O farewell! [*Dies*]

Oth. Why, how should she be murder'd?

Em.   Alas, who knows?

Oth. You heard her say, herself, it was not I.

Em. She said so, I must needs report a truth.

Oth. She 's like a liar gone to burning hell,
'Twas I that kill'd her.

Em.   O, the more angel she,
And you the blacker devil!

Oth. She turn'd to folly, and she was a whore.

Em. Thou dost belie her, and thou art a devil.   140

Oth. She was false as water.

Em.   Thou as rash as fire,
To say that she was false : O, she was heavenly true!

Oth. Cassio did top her, ask thy husband else.
O, I were damn'd beneath all depth in hell,
But that I did proceed, upon just grounds,
To this extremity.   Thy husband knew it all.

Em. My husband?

Oth. Thy husband.

Em. That she was false to wedlock?

Oth. Ay, with Cassio.   Nay, had she been true,   150
If heaven would make me such another world
Of one entire and perfect chrysolite,
I 'ld not have sold her for it.

Em. My husband ?

Oth.   Ay, 'twas he that told me first :
  An honest man he is, and hates the slime
  That sticks on filthy deeds.

Em.   My husband ?

Oth. What needs this iteration ? woman, I say thy husband.

{*Em.* O mistress, villany hath made mocks with love !
  My husband say that she was false !

Oth.   He, woman ;
  I say thy husband : dost understand the word ? 160
  My friend, thy husband, honest, honest Iago.}

Em. If he say so, may his pernicious soul
  Rot half a grain a day ! he lies to the heart :
  She was too fond of her most filthy bargain.

Oth. Ha !

Em. Do thy worst :
  This deed of thine is no more worthy heaven
  Than thou wast worthy her.

Oth.   Peace, you were best.

Em. Thou hast not half the power to do me harm
  As I have to be hurt. O gull, O dolt, 170
  As ignorant as dirt ! thou hast done a deed—
  I care not for thy sword, I 'll make thee know,
  Though I lost twenty lives. Help ! help, ho ! help !
  The Moor has kill'd my mistress ! Murder ! murder !

Enter Montano, Gratiano, Iago, and others

Mon. What is the matter?   How now, general?

Em. O, are you come, Iago? you have done well,
    That men must lay their murders on your neck.

Gra. What is the matter?

Em. Disprove this villain, if thou be'st a man :
    He says thou told'st him that his wife was false ;   180
    I know thou didst not, thou 'rt not such a villain.
    Speak, for my heart is full.

Iago. I told him what I thought, and told no more
    Than what he found himself was apt and true.

Em. But did you ever tell him she was false?

Iago. I did.

Em. You told a lie, an odious, damned lie ;
    Upon my soul, a lie, a wicked lie !
    She false with Cassio ; did you say with Cassio ?

Iago. With Cassio, mistress.   Go to, charm your tongue.   190

Em. I will not charm my tongue ; I am bound to speak :
    {My mistress here lies murder'd in her bed,—

All. O heavens forfend !

Em. And your reports have set the murder on.

Oth. Nay, stare not, masters, it is true indeed.

Gra. 'Tis a strange truth.

Mon. O monstrous act !

Em.   Villany, villany, villany !

I think upon 't : I think : I smell 't : O villany :
I thought so then : I 'll kill myself for grief :
O villany, villany !}   200

Iago. What, are you mad ?   I charge you, get you home.

Em. Good gentlemen, let me have leave to speak,
'Tis proper I obey him, but not now :
Perchance, Iago, I will ne'er go home.

Oth. O ! O ! O !   *Falling on the bed*

Em.   Nay, lay thee down and roar,
For thou hast kill'd the sweetest innocent
That e'er did lift up eye.

Oth.   (*rising*) O, she was foul !
I scarce did know you, uncle : there lies your niece,
Whose breath indeed these hands have newly stopp'd :
I know this act shows terrible and grim.   210

Gra. Poor Desdemona ! I am glad thy father 's dead :
Thy match was mortal to him, and pure grief
Shore his old thread in twain : did he live now,
This sight would make him do a desperate turn,
Yea, curse his better angel from his side,
And fall to reprobation.

Oth. 'Tis pitiful, but yet Iago knows
That she with Cassio hath the act of shame
A thousand times committed ; Cassio confess'd it,
And she did gratify his amorous works   220

With the recognizance and pledge of love
Which I first gave her ; I saw it in his hand,
It was a handkerchief, an antique token
My father gave my mother.

Em. O God !   O heavenly God !

Iago.   'Zounds ! hold your peace.

Em. 'Twill out, 'twill out.   I hold my peace, sir ?   No !
I 'll be in speaking liberal as the air :   †
Let heaven, and men, and devils, let 'em all,
All, all, cry shame against me, yet I 'll speak.

Iago. Be wise, and get you home.

Em.   I will not.

> *Iago offers to stab Emilia*

Gra.   Fie !   230
Your sword upon a woman !

Em. O thou dull Moor, that handkerchief thou speak'st on
I found by fortune, and did give my husband,
For often with a solemn earnestness,
More than indeed belong'd to such a trifle,
He begg'd of me to steal it.

Iago.   Villanous whore !

Em. She gave it Cassio ? no, alas, I found it,
And I did give 't my husband.

Iago.   Filth, thou liest !

Em. By heaven, I do not, I do not, gentlemen.

      O murderous coxcomb ! what should such a fool   240
      Do with so good a woman ?

Oth.   Are there no stones in heaven
      But what serve for the thunder ?   Precious villain !
      He runs at Iago : Iago, from behind, stabs Emilia, and exit

Gra. The woman falls ; sure, he hath kill'd his wife.

Em. Ay, ay : O, lay me by my mistress' side.

Gra. He 's gone, but his wife 's kill'd.

Mon. 'Tis a notorious villain.   Take your weapon,   †
      Which I have here recover'd from the Moor :
      Come, guard the door without, let him not pass,
      But kill him rather.   I 'll after that same villain,
      For 'tis a damned slave.

                    Exeunt all but Othello and Emilia

Oth.   I am not valiant neither,   250
      But every puny whipster gets my sword.
      But why should honour outlive honesty ?
      Let it go all.

Em.   {What did thy song bode, lady ?
      Hark, canst thou hear me ?   I will play the swan,
      And die in music.   (*singing*) Willow, willow, willow.}
      Moor, she was chaste, she lov'd thee, cruel Moor ;
      So come my soul to bliss, as I speak true ;
      So speaking as I think, I die, I die.   *Dies*

Oth. I have another weapon in this chamber,

It is a sword of Spain, the ice-brook's temper ;   260
O, here it is.   Uncle, I must come forth.

Gra. (*within*) If thou attempt it, it will cost thee dear,
Thou hast no weapon, and perforce must suffer.

Oth. Look in upon me then, and speak to me,
Or, naked as I am, I will assault thee.

Re-enter Gratiano

Gra. What is the matter ?

Oth.   Behold, I have a weapon ;
A better never did itself sustain
Upon a soldier's thigh : I have seen the day
That with this little arm, and this good sword,
I have made my way through more impediments   270
Than twenty times your stop : but, O vain boast !
Who can control his fate ? 'tis not so now.
{Be not afraid, though you do see me weapon'd ;
Here is my journey's end, here is my butt
And very sea-mark of my utmost sail.
Do you go back dismay'd ? 'tis a lost fear :
Man but a rush against Othello's breast,
And he retires.   Where should Othello go ?
Now, how dost thou look now ? O ill-starr'd wench !}
Pale as thy smock ! when we shall meet at count,   280
This look of thine will hurl my soul from heaven,
And fiends will snatch at it.   Cold, cold, my girl,

Even like thy chastity.   O cursed slave !
Whip me, you devils,
From the possession of this heavenly sight !
Blow me about in winds, roast me in sulphur,
Wash me in steep-down gulfs of liquid fire !
O Desdemona, Desdemona dead !
Oh ! Oh ! Oh !

Enter Lodovico, Montano, Cassio [carried in a chair,]
and Officers with Iago, prisoner

Lod. Where is this rash and most unfortunate man ?   290
Oth. That 's he that was Othello : here I am.
Lod. Where is this viper ? bring the villain forth.
Oth. I look down towards his feet, but that 's a fable.
   If that thou be'st a devil, I cannot kill thee.

Wounds Iago

Lod. Wring his sword from him.
Iago.   I bleed, sir, but not kill'd.
Oth. I am not sorry neither, I 'ld have thee live,
   For, in my sense, 'tis happiness to die.
Lod. O thou Othello, that wert once so good,
   Fall'n in the practice of a damned slave,
   What should be said to thee ?
Oth.   Why, any thing,   300
   An honourable murderer, if you will ;
   For nought did I in hate, but all in honour.

Lod. This wretch hath part confess'd his villany :
    Did you and he consent in Cassio's death ?

Oth. Ay.

Cas. Dear general, I did never give you cause.

Oth. I do believe it, and I ask you pardon.
    Will you, I pray, demand that demi-devil
    Why he hath thus ensnar'd my soul and body ?

Iago. Demand me nothing ; what you know, you know :   310
    From this time forth I never will speak word.

Lod. What, not to pray ?

Gra.   Torments will ope your lips.

Oth. Well, thou dost best.

Lod. Sir, you shall understand what hath befall'n,
    Which, as I think, you know not.   Here is a letter,
    Found in the pocket of the slain Roderigo ;
    And here another ; the one of them imports
    The death of Cassio ; to be undertook . . .
    By Roderigo.

Oth. O villain !

Cas.   Most heathenish, and most gross !   320

Lod. Now here 's another discontented paper,
    Found in his pocket too, and this, it seems,
    Roderigo meant to have sent this damned villain ;
    But that, belike, Iago in the nick   †
    Came in, and satisfied him.

Oth.   O the pernicious caitiff !
       How came you, Cassio, by a handkerchief
       That was my wife's ?

Cas.   I found it in my chamber,
       And he himself confess'd it even now,
       That there he dropp'd it for a special purpose,
       Which wrought to his desire.

Oth.   O fool, fool, fool !   330

Cas. There is besides in Roderigo's letter,
       How he upbraids Iago, that he made him
       Brave me upon the watch, whereon it came
       That I was cast ; and even but now he spake
       After long seeming dead, Iago hurt him,
       Iago set him on.

Lod. You must forsake this room, and go with us :
       Your power and your command is taken off,
       And Cassio rules in Cyprus.   For this slave,
       If there be any cunning cruelty   340
       That can torment him much, and hold him long,
       It shall be his ; you shall close prisoner rest,
       Till that the nature of your fault be known
       To the Venetian state ; come, bring him away.

Oth. Soft you ; a word or two {before you go.}
       I have done the state some service, and they know 't ;
       No more of that : I pray you, in your letters,

When you shall these unlucky deeds relate,
Speak of them as they are ; nothing extenuate,
Nor set down aught in malice, then must you speak   350
Of one that lov'd not wisely, but too well ;
Of one not easily jealous, but, being wrought,
Perplex'd in the extreme ; of one whose hand,
Like the base Indian, threw a pearl away   †
Richer than all his tribe ; of one whose subdued eyes,
Albeit unused to the melting mood,
Drop tears as fast as the Arabian trees
Their medicinal gum ; set you down this,
And say besides, that in Aleppo once,
Where a malignant and a turban'd Turk   360
Beat a Venetian, and traduc'd the state,
I took by the throat the circumcised dog
And smote him, thus.   [*Stabs himself*]

Lod. O bloody period !

Gra.   All that 's spoke is marr'd.

Oth. I kiss'd thee ere I kill'd thee, no way but this,
Killing myself, to die upon a kiss.

                              Falls on the bed, and dies

Cas. This did I fear, but thought he had no weapon,
For he was great of heart.

Lod.   (*to Iago*) O Spartan dog,
More fell than anguish, hunger, or the sea !

Look on the tragic lodging of this bed ;   †
This is thy work, the object poisons sight,   371
Let it be hid.   Gratiano, keep the house,
And seize upon the fortunes of the Moor ;
For they succeed to you.   To you, lord governor,
Remains the censure of this hellish villain,
The time, the place, the torture : O, enforce it !
Myself will straight aboard, and to the state
This heavy act with heavy heart relate.   *Exeunt*

Notes

I. i. 21. *A fellow almost damn'd in a fair wife*; one of the most famous stumbling-blocks in Shakespeare. The commentators' struggles with it occupy five pages of the Variorum edition. At its face value it means that Cassio is almost damned because he has almost married a fair wife (with allusion to the Italian proverb, 'You have married a fair wife? You are damned'). The allusion must then apparently be to Bianca; and perhaps in spite of various difficulties this is as good an explanation as any, or at least less unsatisfactory than most; but that is not saying much.

I. i. 30. *be-lee'd*; the F reading for Q's *be led*, and perhaps right; but it makes the metre awkward, and I suspect that Shakespeare was coining a word, and as *calm'd* means 'becalmed' meant *be lee'd* to mean 'be belee'd.'

I. i. 33. *worship's*; both F and Q 2 read *Moorship's*, which reads like the work of a would-be clever improver. Iago does not elsewhere show any scorn for Othello's Moorship.

I. i. 158. *the Sagittary*; usually explained as either 'an Inn' or as 'the residence at the Arsenal of the commanding officers of the navy and army.' But Miss V. M. Jeffery has, I think, conclusively shown (*Modern Language Review*, Jan. 1932) that it was Shakespeare's name for a street, the Frezzaria, the street of the arrow-makers.

I. i. 182. *officers of night*; both F and Q 2 read *officers of might*. But this is one of the passages that makes one suspicious of unnecessary departures from Q 1, since the reference is clearly to the 'officers of night' mentioned in Lewkenor's translation of Contareno's *Venice*.

I. ii. 22. *siege*; I leave the traditional reading, which is F's, but

155

hesitatingly; both Quartos read the simple *height*. In the next line *unbonneted* must mean 'without bonnetting,' *i.e.*, without taking off the hat.

I. ii. 78. *For an abuser*; Q 1 *Such an abuser*, clearly joining the cut.

I. iii. 83. *set phrase*; I see no reason to desert this reading of both Quartos for F's *soft*.

I. iii. 157. *beguile her of her tears*; *i.e.*, 'elicit tears from her,' not 'charm away her tears.'

I. iii. 195. The additional Folio line looks at first sight convincing and gives a neat oratorical balance. But in fact the Q 1 reading is surely the better, since Brabantio is as far as may be from giving Desdemona with all his heart.

I. iii. 250. *scorn*; F reads *storme* and Q 2 follows; either reading is graphically easy enough as a misreading of the other; but there seems no reason for involving ourselves in difficult interpretations of *storm*. Two lines lower the same two texts read *very quality*; here I retain Q 1 with more hesitation, since its reading looks suspiciously like a weak alternative for something not well understood. [*Cf. Troilus and Cressida*, I. i. 36, where Q reads *scorn* for *storm*.]

I. iii. 264-65. *Nor to comply* . . .; a famous crux. The reading given is that of Q 1, with omission of comma after *defunct*. F is the same with minor differences of punctuation and spelling, but gives no support to the usual emendation of *me* for *my*. The general sense is so clear (that Othello, now middle-aged, wants the spiritual rather than the physical intercourse) that I do not feel that the pursuit of the commentators is very profitable.

I. iii. 270-71. The reading given is that of Q 1 and Q 2. F reads:

> *Of feather'd Cupid seel with wanton dulness*
> *My speculative and offic'd instrument.*

In either case the sense is clear, but one should not, I think, as many editors have done, combine the two readings. The *speculative and active instruments* (plural) are the mental and physical faculties, the *speculative and offic'd instrument* (singular) is the whole body with brain and limbs.

I. iii. 350. *acerb*; F and Q 2 both *bitter*. It is hard to conceive the transcriber or compositor inserting *acerb* (an uncommon word, since the N.E.D., missing this passage, gives its first occurrence as 1657) unless he had it in his copy.

I. iii. 393. *make up my will, A double knavery*; F reads *plume up my will In double knavery*. Q 2, trying to make the best of both words, reads *plume* but retains *A*, thereby, as is the way of conflations, making the worst.

II. i. 11. *foaming*; this is the easy F and Q 2 reading for Q 1's obscure *banning*, which probably conceals the true reading.

II. i. 55. *governor*; again I take this to be no better than F's easy way with the odd and oddly spelt *guernement* of Q 1 and Q 2.

II. i. 63. The usual reading is to retain the two additional words of F in l. 63, and in l. 65 to read *Does tire the ingener*. One may notice that (*a*) the Q 1 reading is more commonplace; (*b*) that the Q 1 reading will scan with a relineation (*One that excels the blazoning pens, and in | The essential vesture of creation*); (*c*) that the usual reading is not that of F but an emendation of it, since F reads *the Ingeniuer*. The sense of emended F, in spite of the difficulty it has caused, is clear enough; Desdemona, just as God made her, goes beyond the efforts of the most ingenious inventor. This seems a moderately clear case of 'improvement,' and an improvement undeniably in the Shakespearean manner.

II. i. 81. *And swiftly come to*; F reads *Make love's quick pants*;

the alteration is superficially attractive, but the resultant picture is more appropriate to Romeo than Othello.

II. i. 305. *whom I trash*; Q 1 reads *crush*, F and Q 2 *trace*, from neither of which is it easy to extract a tolerable meaning. *Trash*, the usual emendation, is satisfactory in so far as Iago's trouble with Roderigo is normally that the latter is in too much of a hurry, and he has to 'trash' him, *i.e.*, put weights on him to slow him up. One's only hesitation is that at the moment, in contrast to what has been happening before, Iago wants to incite Roderigo.

II. ii. I have retained the punctuation of Q 1, which seems to represent the disjointed utterance of the herald.

II. iii. 13. *Not this hour*; not 'not at this time of night' but 'not for an hour yet'; see the preceding scene, l. 11.

II. iii. 196. *collied*; so F. It is a little suspicious that Q 2 supports the odd reading of Q 1, *coold*; but it does not seem possible to make sense of that.

II. iii. 312. *broken joint*; so both Q 2 and F. Q 1 reads the mysterious *braule*, which certainly will hardly do as it stands, but I suspect it of concealing the true reading.

III. i. 21. *Dost thou hear my honest friend?* This line is an interesting example of the unintelligent tidyings of F, which reads *Dost thou hear me, my honest friend?* thereby making the Clown's answer pointless.

III. iii. 62. *Tuesday morn*; so Q 1. F reads *noon*, perhaps rightly.

III. iii. 152-54. This is an interesting passage with regard to the relation of the three texts. The reading given is that of Q 1. It involves, of course, a complete break and 'pick-up' in syntax. F, wanting to carry on the construction of *I do beseech you* after a parenthesis, reads *Shapes faults that are not—that your wisdom From one that so imperfectly conceits Would take no notice, nor build yourself a trouble Out of his scattering* . . . Q 2 completes the metre by adding *yet* after *wisdom*, but forgets to change *my* to *his*.

III. iii. 170. *which doth mock The meat it feeds on*; there has been a good deal of comment on this, but there is no difficulty so soon as we realise what the picture of jealousy is. We tend to picture jealousy as a malignant power residing in the heart of the jealous man, and from there going out to injure someone else. The picture here is of a power external to the jealous man, so that the meat it feeds on and mocks is his heart.

III. iii. 425. *wary*; so F and Q 2. Q 1 reads *merry*, a quite possible reading.

III. iii. 434. Iag. *'Tis a shrewd doubt.* . . . F and Q 2 give this line to Othello, but the Q 1 distribution seems much more pointed.

III. iv. 46. *But our new heraldry* . . .; on the face of it this seems a clear allusion to a new order of baronets, instituted by the King in 1611, the honour being the addition of a hand gules to the arms; and even if one dislikes the supposition of insertions this seems the most reasonable explanation.

III. iv. 124. *shut myself up*; so F, explained as meaning 'confine myself to.' Q 1 reads *shoote*, and I suspect that the true reading is either *shoot myself upon* (*i.e.*, 'hurry off on') or *suit* (for the 'suit-shoot' pronunciation see *Love's Labour's Lost*, IV. i. 109).

IV. i. 235. *I am glad to see you mad.* An odd remark. The transposition of the two adjectives does not help much, since Othello would hardly use the word 'mad' of himself here, though someone else might use it of him; and to say that he, with whatever emotion, sees her 'mad' does not appear to make sense. It is her 'gladness' that incenses him.

IV. ii. 55-56. *A fixed figure* . . .; so Q 1. F reads *The fixed figure*, and *slow and moving finger*; Q 2 follows Q 1 except for *finger* instead of the plural. There has been a spate of explanation. Some editors support and others dismiss with contumely the idea that Shakespeare is talking in terms of a clock or a sun-dial. I feel that there is no doubt that this is the basis of the metaphor, and that, if Shakespeare had a clock in mind, he is thinking of the imperceptible movement of the hour-hand, if a dial, of the unmoving gnomon and the slow movement of the shadow. In either case I should prefer the singular of Q 2. I cannot agree that 'slow and moving' is a natural Shakespeareanism for 'slowly moving,' because the second word in the phrase is so colourless, whereas in the usual phrases of this type, which are quoted in support, the second word is full of significance.

IV. ii. 63-65. *Turn thy complexion* . . .; the reading given is that of Q 1 and Q 2 with the addition of a comma after *Patience*. F reads *thou* for *thy* with colon after *there* and comma after *Patience*. None of the three texts has the comma after *I* which one would expect if *I* was for *Ay*. In the face of this accord of the three main texts emendation seems to me unjustified, though the reading of *thou* is attractive. *Turn thy complexion* should normally mean 'change colour.' All that I feel clear about is that the *cherubin* means Desdemona. I have wondered in idle moments whether there may have been a mirror, in which Othello saw the contrast between Desdemona's youthful loveliness and his own grim face. But in any case we are left with the awkward apostrophe to *Patience*.

IV. ii. 111. *greatest abuse*; so Q 1. F reads *least misuse*, a characteristic reading, appearing to be a regularisation, and in fact weakening the point. Desdemona's point surely is that even if he takes her *greatest* misdemeanour he cannot justly stick the smallest opinion on it.

IV. ii. 150. *O good Iago*; (Q 1, *O Good Iago*). F's reading, *Alas*

Iago, rather suggests that it took the original to be *O God, Iago*; as perhaps it was.

IV. ii. 172. *And the great messengers* . . .; so Q 1. Some curious things happen here. F reads *The messengers of Venice staies the meate*, which is at least a good enough line. One imagines that the compositor of Q 2 got muddled with the deletions and insertions in his copy, since the line appears as *The meate, great messengers of Venice stay.* The confusion at first sight looks as though it might support the view that Q 2 had some relation to a difficult MS., but I think on experiment it will be seen that the most natural explanation is that the compositor (working from a corrected copy of Q 1) confused the deletion of *And the great* with the place for the insertion of *the meate*.

V. i. 14. *makes my gain*; Q reads *makes my game*, and I should like to retain it, since it is on the face of it a more vivid phrase, in some such sense as ' gives me the game '; but I cannot find any support for this in N.E.D., and so reluctantly yield to F and tradition. The difference between *gaine* and *game* is, of course, graphically negligible.

V. i. 86. *To bear a part in this*; so Q 1. F reads *To be a party in this injury*; Q 2 tries to combine, and reads *To bear a part in this injury*, which will not even scan. I suspect that the true reading is that of Q 1, but with the omission of *good Cassio*. We then get a good line, *To bear a part in this*; *patience awhile*; and as Cassio appears to have fainted there is no point in telling *him* to be patient. If *good Cassio* had then crept in the Folio would be at its usual trick of regularising, by expanding one line and inserting *Come, come* in the next.

V. i. 105. *good gentlemen*; so F. Both Quartos read *good gentlewoman*, as though addressed to Bianca. But it is an unnatural way for Iago to address Bianca. In the following lines I give, with some hesitation, the reading of the two Quartos; F reads *gastness, stare,* and *hear.*

V. i. 114. *and Roderigo dead*; the point is of no intrinsic importance, but worth perhaps recording as illustrating the strange results of F's desire for precision; F reads *and Roderigo quite dead!*

V. ii. 74. *he hath . . . us'd thee*; Q 1 has the remarkable reading *he hath . . . uds death.* The sudden break would be effective and in character, and one might accept it if it were not that it leaves Desdemona's rejoinder with no point of reference.

V. ii. 227. *liberal as the air*; so Q 1. F and Q 2 *liberal as the north,* which has evoked long comments and is indeed obscure. One would accept Q 1 without question except that it is hard to see why anyone with the simple *ayre* in front of him should go out of his way to emend to *north.*

V. ii. 246. *your weapon*; so Q 1 and 2. F *you this weapon.* The variant is a good deal more interesting than on the surface it appears. If Q 1 is right the stage business must be that Othello is not himself armed and draws Gratiano's sword for his attack on Iago. This suits well enough with the natural supposition that Montano and Gratiano, who have entered in response to a cry of 'Murder,' have entered armed. It suits less well, however, with Othello's 'my sword' and 'another weapon.'

V. ii. 324, 326. *nick; a handkerchief*; two perfect examples of the operations of F. First it gets rid of a colloquialism at the cost of two extra syllables which wreck the run of the line, and reads *in the interim.* Then it finds *a* weak for the handkerchief about which there has been so much talk, and reads *that,* which is dramatically quite wrong, since Cassio has not been present at the previous discussion and to him it is just *a* handkerchief, the handkerchief whose unexpected presence in his room had puzzled him.

V. ii. 354. *base Indian*; so both Quartos. Why any editor should want to read *Judean*, with F, except as an occasion for long notes that the Judean is probably Herod who discarded Mariamne, or possibly Judas Iscariot, is one of the mysteries of criticism. If there were no F reading to trouble us, surely no reader would have hesitated for a moment in assuming that we have here an allusion presumably to a current traveller's tale about some nameless Indian who threw away in sheer ignorance a valuable pearl.

V. ii. 370. *lodging*; so Q 1. Editors have almost universally accepted F's *loading*. But Q 2 found no difficulty with Q 1's *lodging*, and 'lodge' is good Elizabethan for 'beat down,' as a storm beats down standing corn (as in *Macbeth* IV. i. 55, *Though bladed corn be lodg'd*). Of the two pictures that of the Qq. is considerably the more vivid.

Glossary

MANY words and phrases in Shakespeare require glossing, not because they are in themselves unfamiliar, but for the opposite reason, that Shakespeare uses in their Elizabethan and unfamiliar sense a large number of words which seem so familiar that there is no incentive to look for them in the glossary. It is hoped that a glossary arranged as below will make it easy to see at a glance what words and phrases in any particular scene require elucidation. A number of phrases are glossed by what seems to be, in their context, the modern equivalent rather than by lexicographical glosses on the words which compose them.

Act First

SCENE I

line
10 CAPP'D, took cap off
13 BOMBAST CIRCUMSTANCE, padded circumlocution
16 NONSUITS, denies suit of
19 ARITHMETICIAN, technical expert
23 DIVISION, disposition
24 UNLESS, unless it be
25 TOGED CONSULS, civil councillors robed in the toga
27 HAD THE ELECTION, was chosen
31 COUNTER-CASTER, arithmetician
32 IN GOOD TIME, *ironic*, 'forsooth!'
33 ANCIENT, ensign
36 LETTER, testimonial
39 AFFIN'D, bound

line
50 VISAGES, masks
63 COMPLEMENT EXTERN, outside show
66 OWE, own
73 AS, that
100 UPON . . . BRAVERY, 'being above yourself'
101 START, startle
106 GRANGE, lonely country house
113 GENNET, Spanish horse
     GERMANS, relations
123 ODD-EVEN, midnight (*as though* '*turn of the tide*')
127 YOUR ALLOWANCE, sanctioned by you
131 FROM, contrary to
136 EXTRAVAGANT, vagrant

164

Act I   Sc. i—*continued*

line
149 CAST, discard
152 FATHOM, (*mod. met. would be*) calibre
NIGHTGOWN, dressing-gown

line
183 I'LL DESERVE YOUR PAINS, *i.e.* you'll lose nothing by any trouble you take for me

SCENE II

5 YERK'D, dug
21 PROVULGATE, publish
22 DEMERITS, merits
23 UNBONNETED, not taking cap off
49 ANCIENT, ensign

50 CARACK, large merchantman
77 ATTACH, arrest
79 INHIBITED, prohibited
82 MY INCLINING, my party
89 PAGANS, barbarians

SCENE III

1 COMPOSITION, coherence
5 JUMP ON, agree in
10 SECURE ME TO THE ERROR, insist on the inaccuracy
19 PAGEANT, display
91 ROUND, plain
108 TEST, evidence
109 THIN HABITS, mere appearances
110 MODERN, trivial
141 ANTRES, caves
IDLE, empty
155 BY PARCEL, bit by bit
156 INTENTIVELY, continuously
190 GOD BU'Y, good-bye
201 GREESE, step
210 BOOTLESS, profitless
220 PIERCED, touched
225 ALLOWED, recognised
226 VOICE, choice

227 SLUBBER, cloud
232 AGNIZE, recognise in myself
239 BESORT, fitting company
260 DEAR, deeply felt
273 SKILLET, small saucepan
274 INDIGN, unworthy
283 QUALITY OR RESPECT, sort or kind
286 CONVEYANCE, escort
290 DELIGHTED, admired
324 GENDER, kind
DISTRACT, (?) diversify
326 CORRIGIBLE, correcting
331 MOTIONS, impulses
332 STINGS, passions
333 SECT, cutting ('*scion*' is practically synonymous)
339 PERDURABLE, perpetual
340 STEAD, support

165

Act I Sc. iii—*continued*

line

341 DEFEAT THY FAVOUR, disguise your face

USURP'D, assumed

349 LOCUSTS, (*a*) fruit of carob tree, or (*b*) honeysuckle

line

350 COLOQUINTIDA, a bitter drug

368 HEARTED, heart-felt

373 TRAVERSE, get busy

393 MAKE UP, complete

397 DISPOSE, disposition

Act Second

SCENE I

2 FLOOD, surge

9 HOLD THE MORTISE, remain jointed

19 BEAR IT OUT, come through it

23 SUFFERANCE, disaster

49 OF VERY EXPERT AND APPROV'D ALLOWANCE, generally allowed to be expert

63 QUIRKS, flourishes

70 GUTTER'D, channelled

71 ENSTEEP'D, immersed

77 FOOTING, landing

78 SE'NNIGHT, week

111 BELLS, chatterers

127 FREEZE, rough tweed

139 FOND, foolish

164 PROFANE, coarse

165 LIBERAL, libertine

167 IN, ' qua '

175 PLAY THE SIR, play the gallant

178 CLYSTER-PIPES, enema-pipes

201 SET DOWN THE PEGS, slacken the strings

214 PRESENTLY, straight away

230 FAVOUR, face

237 PREGNANT, natural

238 POSITION, premise

240 CONSCIONABLE, conscientious

246 NEVER, *sc.* which never

248 GREEN, callow

252 CONDITION, disposition

270 TAINTING, carping at

277 QUALIFICATION, state of mind

278 TRUST, trustfulness

SCENE III

14 CAST, discarded

37 CRAFTILY QUALIFIED, prudently watered down

58 CONSEQUENCE, the event

APPROVE, realise

60 ROUSE, health

Act II Sc. iii—*continued*

line	*line*
85 LOWN, loon	208 PARTIALLY AFFIN'D, bound by
122 HOROLOGE A DOUBLE SET, two	partiality
rounds of the clock	263 CAST, cast off
140 WICKER, cased in wicker	294 HYDRA, many-headed monster of
144 MAZZARD, head	Greek mythology
170 IN QUARTER, on good terms	298 INGREDIENCE, ingredients
175 PEEVISH ODDS, senseless quarrel	314 LAY, odds
183 CENSURE, judgment	328 PROBAL, probable
185 OPINION, reputation	354 FILLS UP THE CRY, *i.e.* is in the
196 COLLIED, darkened	pack for voice alone, not
200 ROUT, uproar	scent
	376 JUMP, just

Act Third

SCENE I

12 OF ALL LOVES, ' for any sake '	43 DISPLEASURE, disfavour
23 QUILLETS, tricky jests (*quid-*	47 OF GREAT AFFINITY, well-con-
libets)	nected

SCENE III

16 BREED ITSELF SO OUT OF CIR-	139 TO, *i.e.* not to do
CUMSTANCE, so increase by	144 LEETS, ' petty sessions '
accidents	177 FINELESS, limitless
19 DOUBT, suspect	202 SECURE, carefree
23 WATCH, keep him awake	204 SELF-BOUNTY, generosity
TAME, into tameness	214 SEEL, close (*met. from sewing up*
24 SHRIFT, confessional	*bawks' eyes*)
27 SOLICITOR, advocate	CLOSE AS OAK, *i.e. because close-*
67 NOT ALMOST, hardly	*grained*)
75 IN, back into favour	233 AFFECT, favour
119 CONCEIT, conception	234 COMPLEXION, ' colour '
124 STOPS, hesitations	DEGREE, rank

Act III Sc. iii—*continued*

line
238 IN POSITION, with positive affirmation
264 HAGGARD, wild hawk
265 JESSES, leather straps by which hawk was held
269 CHAMBERERS, 'ladies' men'
280 FORKED PLAGUE, *i.e.* the cuckold's horns
291 NAPKIN, handkerchief
300 TA'EN OUT, copied
303 FOR, in accordance with
331 CONCEITS, imaginations

line
335 MANDRAGORA, mandrake (*considered an opiate*)
338 OW'DST, hadst
351 PIONERS, 'sappers and miners'
370 HINGE (*cf. 'hanging' a gate*)
404 BOLSTER, go to bed
408, 409 PRIME, PROUD, 'on heat'
453 FRAUGHT, freight
454 ASPICS', asps'
468 CLIP, encircle
472 REMORSE, duty

SCENE IV

2 LIES, lodges
25 CRUSADOES, Portuguese gold coins (stamped with Cross)
30 HUMOURS, moods, vapours
39 SEQUESTER FROM LIBERTY, confinement
50 RHEUM, cold
58 EGYPTIAN, gipsy
72 SIBYL, seeress
74 FURY, inspiration
76 MUMMY, magical preparation from mummies

131 BLANK, aim
144 UNHATCH'D PRACTICE, hidden treason
146 PUDDLED, muddied
159 TOY, trifle
172 MAKE YOU, are you doing
183 TAKE OUT, copy
197 ADDITION, credit
204 BE CIRCUMSTANC'D, be a creature of circumstance

Act Fourth

SCENE I

28 CONVINCED OR SUPPLIED, overcome or satisfied (*corresponding to 'importunate suit' and 'voluntary dotage'*)

63 HORNED MAN, cuckold
67 YOK'D, married
69 UNPROPER, not exclusively their own

Act IV Sc. i—*continued*

line

70 PECULIAR, their own
72 SECURE, unsuspecting
76 LIST, limit
80 ECSTASY, madness
81 RETIRE, return
102 CONSTER, construe
105 ADDITION, title
120 CUSTOMER, prostitute

line

127 SCOR'D, branded, *or* scored a point
145 FITCHEW, polecat
149-50 TAKE OUT, copy
153-54 HOBBY-HORSE, 'light-o'-love'
208 BE HIS UNDERTAKER, 'look after him'
229 ATONE, reconcile

SCENE II

123 CALLET, drab
134 COGGING, tricking
COZENING, cheating
141 ABUS'D, deluded
143 COMPANIONS, rascals
146 WITHIN DOORS, low

147 SQUIRE, fellow
177 DOFF, put off
181 PUT UP, pocket up
190 A VOTARIST, a 'religious'
196 FOPP'D, cheated

SCENE III

20 CHECKS, reproofs
32 BUT TO GO, not to go
73 JOINT-RING, jointed ('gimmal') ring

73 LAWN, fine linen
76 EXHIBITION, present
84 TO THE VANTAGE, besides

Act Fifth

SCENE I

11 QUAT, 'pimple'

16 BOBB'D cheated

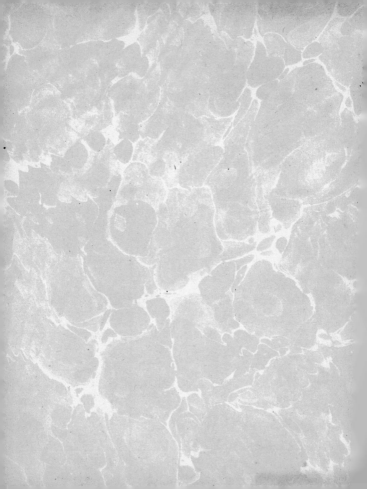